Not in the History Books

by Hugh Delamere

Copyright © 2016 Hugh Delamere
All rights reserved. No part of this text may be reproduced, photocopied or otherwise used in any way without the prior written approval and consent of Hugh Delamere.

ISBN# 978-9966-7572-8-9
Published by Old Africa Books
A division of Kifaru Educational and Editorial Consultants LTD
PO Box 2338-20117, Naivasha, Kenya

Illustrations by Bea Armstrong of Gilgil. Used by permission.

Author's Preface

I have always been interested in History, which has formed us into what we are today. But I am most interested in how people behaved, what they thought, and what they knew, compared with today.

But, frustratingly, History as taught in schools used to be a list of dates of Monarchs and battles, with very little about the actual people. It has now improved, but there are still gaps. My collection of vignettes may be imaginary, invented or untrue, but it is my best attempt at filling some gaps.

Hugh Delamere, Soysambu, Kenya 2016

Darwin

Many years ago but long after the dinosaurs had disappeared, all ones ancestors lived in Russia and the reason they couldn't live in Britain was that it was covered in ice. Everybody's ancestors originated in Africa, which was rather hot, and people left by various means. There were several routes out of Africa, not all of them very appealing. However, people scattered round the world remarkably quickly and quite a few people found there were good things to eat up near the edge of the ice caps, which of course were halfway down Russia. Mammoths were a good thing to eat because if you could frighten them into a crevasse they would get stuck and you could spear them and cut them up and eat them. The main difficulty with living is that nobody had invented houses and so they had to live in caves. It was curious but there was a shortage of caves in Africa but there were a few caves to be had in most of Russia. Getting a good cave was really important like finding a good school for your children. So people lived in caves and they hunted mammoths and the grandfather of the tribe, the eldest chap in it, who might be something really senior like 35 years old, would naturally take the best bit of the cave which was up at the narrow end. Now caves taper, they get wider towards the mouth and they look very much like the gramophone horn on the label of His Master's Voice records. The reason for the gramophone horn is that if you make a little, tinny scratching noise at the narrow end it gets louder and louder as it gets down to the wide end.

In those days one hibernated because it snowed and was pitch dark for six months a year. Catching mammoths had to be organised. The women of course drove the men out to go hunting by the time it came round to about August they said "Look we haven't had a mammoth for some time, winter is going to come on in about a month. You better go out and get something". So what they used to do – they hadn't got pottery or baskets or anything – they had a leather bag (which were like a goatskin that you would keep wine or water in today in some parts) and the women would go out and pick a whole load of blueberries and boysenberries, and whatever kind of berry grew there, and they'd chew them up and spit them into these leather bags where they'd ferment. "Right!" they would say to the men. "Now here's your energy rations. You will off and go hunting and don't forget to come back with a mammoth! Otherwise you'll be hungry and die in the winter." So the men would take these bags of fermented liquor with great joy and they disappeared over the horizon carrying their spears, which of course had a flint tip as obsidian was less readily available in Russia but flint was available. Having got well out of sight of the cave where the women and children were, they get into a clump of bushes and they sit down, they drink the booze, they sleep it off for a day or two then they come back saying "Terribly sorry we couldn't find any mammoths and we've run out of booze."

Of course the women were expecting this and gave them another lot of booze and said, "This time, we're not going to let you back in the cave if you don't come back with a mammoth." However, in time no doubt they did come back with a mammoth and obviously they did because we wouldn't be here today if our ancestors hadn't survived.

You and I and everybody – well all the white races – lived in the middle of Russia. You couldn't live in places like Norway or Sweden or England because they were under thousands of feet of ice. In fact the clay in Sussex today was the southern end of where the glaciers started to melt a little bit and dropped out all the finely ground stone flour which of course is clay. They learnt to make mammoth ham and granddad would have one of these, just a medium sized one, hanging on a stout oak peg about four inches thick hammered into a crack in the wall up the narrow end of the cave. Every time he woke up he would cut a slice off with his flint and chew it and go to sleep again for another fortnight and, well, a big slice of mammoth ham takes a couple of days to eat. Making the ham is quite complicated but that is really a different story and boiling it was probably how they invented pottery.

There are several theories about the invention of pottery and the one that I've always subscribed to was that people wanted to make baskets waterproof so to begin with they lined them with sheep's fat and when that started to leak they said, "To hell with that! Let's line it with clay which is thicker." So they made a basket which would indeed hold water.

They make such things in Africa to this day. But occasionally they'd fall into the fire and they'd get burnt and then the clay sets, its baked hard, and on it of course is the pattern of the basket or sometimes it is a sort of woven cloth bag from one of the wild fibres that grows in Africa. There's some proof of this because a lot of the pottery that's made to this day by some of the tribes (I particularly mention in Africa because I'm not familiar with so many other places) have patterns on them, inscribed, which look rather like basketwork or woven stuff. It seems a sort of feature of those different tribes' cultures that they have different patterns, so they could have invented pottery like that.

I have yet another theory. How on earth did they invent the early Alibaba jar? Big enough to hold a man, if you remember? The truth is, I believe, they invented those when they had to boil a mammoth ham. What they would do is to dig a hole in the floor of the cave. Now the floor of the cave was covered with old chips of flints, old ashes and bits of bone, thoroughly un-waterproof. So they'd dig a decent hole, maybe five or six feet deep, and then they'd line it with clay and hope that it was going to be waterproof which it was to a certain extent. Then, when they'd caught their mammoth, they'd make a wooden tripod and fill up the hole with water, or nearly fill it with water, lower the ham into it (Archimedes discovered that baths overflow if they're full and you then get into it and no doubt they noticed the same effect). Then they kept all the children busy (tremendous group activities in those days).

Everybody had to join in or they'd all have starved. There'd be a huge fire roaring outside the cave and they'd put rocks in it. Then with the aid of two branches of green wood like alder or something or even willow they'd take a red hot rock and drop it into this clay lined hole which had a mammoth ham hanging in it. When you'd dropped enough red hot rocks in (they soon learnt to make the hole much larger than the mammoth ham because you had to have room for the rocks), the water started to boil and as it was down in a well-insulated place, surrounded with old ashes and bones and chips and things, it stayed pretty hot for a very long time and the children were detailed off to throw in the odd rock to keep it just simmering nicely. You see, to cook a ham is like cooking a stew. You don't really have to boil it; you want to simmer it because if you do actually boil it, it just gets tougher. If you keep it below boiling point, but hot, it cooks gently and gradually and the heat gets all through it. With mammoth ham you have to keep it hot for some days so the heat gets right through the middle. The purpose of doing this of course is to preserve it and stop it just rotting away. There were problems of course getting food in winter in a cave, even when you've stocked up with mammoth ham and things.

The women and children would be out near the entrance where there were usually barriers, stones, almost a wall and on top of that would be a mass of thorn bushes. The idea and the intention of this was to keep out the sabre-toothed sheepdogs, which were extremely dangerous and nine foot high at the shoulder. They would come up, sniffing round these caves, and probably leap over the barrier because, unfortunately, due to the shortage of firewood under the thick snow, the women tended to use up the thorn barriers for cooking. Well, that's quite understandable. Granddad was right up the narrow end, you see, snoring. The snore was amplified by the His Master's Voice gramophone effect and by the time it reached the outside, where these really very intelligent sheep dogs (I mean, sheepdogs are very intelligent) are debating whether to spring over the barrier, grab somebody, run away and eat it, they could hear this most awful noise (which I can't produce in typing, but was a snort, a gasp, a roar, a growl, a genuine proper adult snore) booming down the cave and this would frighten them away. Now, they're very interesting animals, the sabre-toothed sheepdogs, because they have such furry feet they didn't even leave tracks on snow and certainly nothing in mud. The absence of the footprints of the sabre-toothed sheepdog helps confirm the truth of my story. What's more, when they died they would immediately be snapped up by the hyenas and perhaps the sabre-toothed tigers, which undoubtedly are the things that helped corroborate the whole thing.

That story was essential, but I haven't quite got back to the way they invented the Alibaba jar. Occasionally the children would get out of hand and hadn't noticed that the water had all boiled away around the ham. In fear of a flogging, they would carry on heaving red hot stones into this pit and in the end there would be a strong smell of burnt, charred meat and bones and the red hot stones would bake the clay and whereupon, no longer being slightly plastic, it would leak. So they waited until everything had cooled down and then three or four of the children would hold another one by their ankles and hold him or her upside down to start fishing out the stones once they had got cold. It could take days if there was a whole heap of red hot stones. Then, once you'd poured in some water to cool the stones down a bit, you'd find that the clay at the side had cracked because it had got hard. By the time you'd finished pulling out all the stones you can imagine granddad was belting everybody with strips of mammoth hide, which made quite a good whip. I don't know how good their vocabulary was in those days, but he was probably pretty emphatic. "You idle little brutes," he would say and whack! Eventually they'd pull all the stones out and he'd send them down with some more clay to fill in the cracks so the next time they boiled ham it'd be waterproof.

You didn't get a mammoth every day; they were big lumbering things and they used to move miles looking for food. They had a hell of a bad time in the winter; they used to beat down through the snow. That's why they had such long tusks, to try and eat pathetic little tiny things like arctic willows that grow there underneath the snow, sometimes six foot down. However, they survived and mammoths went on for thousands of years. The last one died out, oh I don't know, fifteen or twenty thousand years ago, so quite recently really. Fresh ivory is still found from the mammoths. So that's one way of inventing pottery, but snoring was an essential survival factor because otherwise we wouldn't have had any ancestors. They would all have been eaten by sabre-toothed sheepdogs.

Alfred the Bad Cook

King Alfred the Bad Cook reorganised England very thoroughly. In his day there were a lot of Danes running about pillaging and the locals resented it. So Alfred the Bad Cook decided to put an alderman in every hundred. A hundred of course wasn't a parish it was a hundred taxable hearths, it might contain two or three parishes, and an alderman was somebody responsible who had probably been heavily lamed in a battle with the Danes. If you have seen Burne Jones's pictures, no doubt you'll imagine he was a man in shining armour upon a fine grey horse, but wearing plate armour. However, in Alfred the Bad Cook's reign plate armour had not been invented and Burne Jones hadn't been born.

Alfred had a funny way of spelling and his idea of spelling alderman is e-a-o-r-l-d-e-r- m-a-n and of course their job was to blow a trumpet, not as in Burne Jones's pictures a Boosey and Hawkes's gold-plated brass three valve trumpet, but the fact is he would have had a cow horn and if he saw any Danes raping anybody or doing a bit of pillaging he was meant to gallop to the top of the hill and blow his horn. In order for him to get to the top of the hill, considering he'd been heavily lamed in a previous battle with the Danes, it was necessary that he should have transport, but Burne Jones got it slightly wrong. He would not have been on an enormous grey charger. With a bit of luck - if he'd be lucky, very lucky - he might have had a donkey, but if he wasn't quite as lucky he was assisted up the hill by a large billy goat.

The English language in those days was not exactly the same as it is today. In fact if you saw some written English in those days it looks like gibberish. But the word swic (to have a drink) was in constant use in those days, because they were just as thirsty as they are now, and to drink was to swicca (the first c has an accent over it, indicating it was pronounced as a g) - which in modern English is to have a swig - but nevertheless it was difficult to understand.

To show somebody was a person in authority they had to wear the right clothes in those days. The alderman had to wear fur, and he had to wear fur both summer and winter. Probably the only fur he could afford was a sheepskin jacket with the fur inside and of course he put an old sack over himself if it was snowing.

Nonetheless there were some various forms of misuse of language which were popular even in the reign of King Alfred the Bad Cook. The Danes did their best at raping, pillaging, house burning, tripping other people and interesting things but they did them in the summer so they didn't get frostbite. The poor alderman had to wear his fur jackets summer and winter, get to the top of the hill and blow his cowhorn.

Some people learned to pay attention of course and joined up in the fyrrd. The purpose of the fyrrd was to chop up the Danes and not just the Danes, but anybody such as the Vikings who would steal things. Alfred actually had considerable successes against the Danes.

There were several specific uses of words derived from swicca. Like the word swuggy. You could say, "It's a rather swuggy day today," but that wasn't what they used the word for in the days of King Alfred the Bad Cook. The word swuggy had a particular meaning and what it meant was, especially in August, "in an alderman's armpit."

The Wizard Michael Scott

The wizard Michael Scott was a figure of Scottish myth but there was no doubt he was also a real person. The legends about him say that he fell asleep on a little knowe; a knowe is a little hummock in Scotland covered in grass, which is usually part of the terminal moraine of a glacier. At any rate he fell asleep on a knowe and when he woke up he found it had opened and was the gate to fairyland. He could hear a song and dance going on inside and it sounded really jolly so he went in. He was met by the queen of the fairies who was extremely well dressed and very nice to him and said, "Do come in and have dinner with us. Afterwards there will be a little dancing, I'm sure you'd enjoy that."

So Michael said, "Thank you very much Ma'am, yes indeed. What's your name?"

"Well, I'm the Queen of the Fairies" she replied. So he had a thoroughly good evening and he went, eventually, through the doorway of fairyland back onto the knowe and sat down, fell asleep and when he woke the door had disappeared.

Some villagers came by and said, "Goodness, you've been gone for seven years!"

"No," he said, "I've only been gone for one night. I was in fairyland."

Now, that is the myth, but the truth of the story is during the seven years that he appeared to be missing, he had actually gone off on a crusade. I don't know if this was the first crusade, which was about 1096, or the second one in 1145. Either way it's a fairly antique story. Nevertheless, he collected a legend about him because when he came back from the crusade he'd got a great, big, thick book in Arabic which was actually the Almagest. It was thick with pages on medicine. The Arabs had some idea of medicine but at that time the people in Europe had none. They regarded the whole thing as witchcraft, but the Arabs had written this great book about medicine called the Almagest, which of course was all in Arabic. None of the locals could read it; they couldn't read anything, but they could tell it wasn't in the sort of writing they expected to find in the Bible, so they assured themselves this man must be a wizard. They didn't burn him at the stake or anything, but they attributed powers to him, which he probably didn't possess. They said that he had a remarkable facility for setting a broken leg, putting it in a splint and binding it up and making the chap keep still until it got better along with various other things like one or two fevers he could cure with certain herbs whose names he knew probably in Arabic.

There are various other stories told about him but I like the ones my grandfather told me. He said one night Michael Scott wasn't sleeping very well. I think the truth was he'd been up at North Berwick and had had a damn good lobster dinner, which as I'm sure you know is completely indigestible. Anyway the Devil appeared to him in a dream and said unless you can set me to work so that I can go forever I will steal your soul. The wizard Michael Scott was in fact a Christian and didn't want his soul stolen so he said to the Devil, "Divide the Eildon hill into three." Now the Eildon hills are very near St Boswells, which nowadays is just known to be a small railway station but back then it was a small town. The Eildon hill is in fact three very precisely similar volcanic cones. They're not particularly big and they belong to a relation of mine who has planted them up with pine trees which has kept them in very good order. They're absolutely identical and are in a straight line, nearly touching.

In the story the hill was only one and the Devil was told to divide them into three, which he did with no trouble at all. In the morning there were three absolutely identical Eildon hills, so the next night when the Devil appeared to the wizard Michael Scott, who had obviously been eating a lot of lobster, the Devil said, "Well, I finished that in one night. Now give me something to keep me busy or I'll take your soul." So Michael said, "Dam the Tweed." He didn't specify the terms exactly and there is a great lava dyke across the Tweed just inland from where it runs into the sea at Berwick and apparently the Devil put it up in one night. It's a big lava dyke and the river runs over it like a waterfall. So the next night the Devil came back to see Michael, who must have had endless supplies of lobster. It was probably his favourite food. I always think putting cheese on it ruins it, but he might have had it lobster thermidor.

By this time Michael was really worried about his soul and he said, "Right, I've got a job for you. Plait the sands of the Solway into rope." The Devil went away and he hasn't been back since. Now if you look at the estuary of the Solway there are big flat sands at lowtide with little, weaving tide lines in the sand from where the last wave of the retreating tide washed up some extra sand and it does look very like layers of string laid out to be woven. However, being only sand, you can't pick them up and weave them so the Devil is still at it and Michael Scott got away; his soul is safe. I forget where he is buried but as you can tell from the places mentioned that he lived in South Scotland. This is the place where my ancestors came from and indeed I was brought up there as a child listening to all these wonderful tales and legends. But the Romans called the Eildon Hills 'Trimontium' or the Triple Hill.

To Knowing How

In 1601 the old Queen was pretty sick and in the same year a youth was apprenticed to a clock maker in London. In 1604 there was a hell of a gale and it blew off the minute hand, the great long minute hand, on the clock in Salisbury. By 1608 the apprentice had finished his indenture and was a master clock maker in his own right. He set out with a leather bag of tools over his shoulder, most of which he'd made during his apprenticeship. He had all sort of vital tools and devices; dividers, callipers, things for spacing the teeth on gear wheels or accurately drilling the holes for spindles and a little tiny, tiny lathe which he turned by hand and was the only way of making clock spindles. He set off pushing for work because he'd just finished his seven years apprenticeship and was now considered an expert. He was indeed; he could engrave designs on brass plates to make the faces of clocks of all sizes because they didn't have wristwatches in those days. Although Charles the First had a wristwatch which he gave to Bishop Juxon on the scaffold when they cut his head off in 1649, but that was a rarity. It came into the possession of my family but my father sold it to pay his gambling debts.

Anyway, this young clock maker set off and couldn't find any work near London so he kept walking further and further west and eventually he arrived at Salisbury, which has a large cathedral. He peered up at the spire, which was 404 feet high and was for a time the tallest building in Britain. Tall and very narrow, on one side of it was a clock face. However, the minute hand was missing; it had been blown off in the gale of 1604. Well, this young clocksmith with his rather heavy bag of tools over his shoulder approached the cathedral where he found one of the vergers cutting the grass near the foot of the tower.

He said, "Your clock's not keeping very good time," to which the verger replied, "Arrr."

So he replied "The reason it's not keeping good time is the minute hand is missing," and the verger said "Arrr."

"Well," he said, "it happens I'm a clock mender by trade and I could put the minute hand back on for you and get the clock keeping good time." To which the verger replied, "Arrr."

This wasn't helpful to the Londoner so he said to the verger, "Do you want the clock mended?"

The verger said "Oi'll have to ashk the chapter, they sit every Wednesday and today by chance is a Wednesday so Oi'll go in and ashk 'em." So the verger disappeared for half an hour and when he came out again he said, "Arrr, they would like the clock repaired."

The clocksmith said "Have you got the hand? It was about 10 feet long."

"Can't find it nowhere."

"What about the nut that held it onto the spindle?"

"Can't be found neither."

"Right, so I'll have to make a new hand and a new nut. I'll have to get up to the spindle of this clock." It was on the outside face of one side of the spire and very difficult to get at. There was no way up the inside that would lead you within an arm's length of the clock. The works were inside the tower but the face of it was outside and there wasn't even a ledge wide enough for a pigeon to sit on. So he went down into the town and inspected all the ladders he could find, walked up and down them and then hired them. He needed a great deal of rope so he tested every piece of rope he could find in the town and hired that. Then he thought a few small boys might be useful so he hired a couple of those. He paid quite high wages for a small boy in Salisbury – over a penny a week!

Eventually he got the ladders lashed to the tower, having tested every piece of rope to see it wouldn't break. The ladders were all tied to each other as well and every ladder had a rope round it to hold it to the tower. The town was definitely feeling a bit short of rope. He ascended up this great mass of ladders to the clock face, which was set very high. He measured the spindle, which was just as he thought a standard English figure two inches. There was a thread on it, which was a standard four threads to the inch, which was a size much used by clock makers in those days. Of course, taps and dies hadn't really been invented for large materials like three inch steel nuts. Dies had been invented to a certain extent because most small house clocks were made of two parallel plates of brass held apart by spacers which in turn had little bolts on them which held the two plates parallel and equidistant apart. Between them were all the spindles and gear and all that sort of thing. However, when it comes to a three inch nut, that was a different matter. Having measured the spindle, he went down to the black smith and ordered a suitable lump of iron to make the nut. Nuts in those days were square not hexagonal and he got the blacksmith to bore a hole through the middle that was the lesser diameter of the threads. While that was being done he went round the town and he bought a bar of copper ten feet long. He worked on it with his chisels, which were in his tool bag, and he cut Time's Arrow into this bar of copper, filed it nicely and polished it then took it to the goldsmith and had it gilded; that was the most expensive part of the operation.

In the meantime he got two small boys putting pegs out at the foot of the tower; he wanted the shortest possible shadow to know when local midday was. He was a very well educated young man. He didn't realise, of course, that when the electric telegraph came in some centuries later the time was the same in Salisbury as it was in London; it would be called railway time, but without the telegraph you just had to take the time from local midday. To get a clock reasonably accurate on local midday, you had to know when local midday was, which was when the shadow of the sticks was the shortest.

The townspeople were getting very interested in this and they gathered, I wouldn't say in large crowds as most of them had work to do, but a lot of people saw what he was doing. When he'd been there four or five days, he carried this great length of copper up the face of the tower and put it on the clock face, tested it, fitted it and carried it down again. Then he went back to the blacksmith who'd produced this lump of iron. Cutting a thread inside the lump is very difficult without taps and dies. What he did was, having measured the pitch of the thread with the aid of his callipers and one thing and another, he divided the perimeter into 32 parts, which he could do very nicely because he was good at geometry. He was able to calculate the pitch of the thread down from the surface of the nut and scribed this inside the hole and then chiselled out the hollow bit of the thread; in a nut that big there are about three or four turns of it. He chiselled it out and got it looking nice and then he had to keep climbing up and down this terrible assembly of ladders to check that the nut did indeed fit. First he got it on one turn, then he got it on all three turns, then he made a copper lock washer, brought up the minute hand, fitted it onto the spindle and twiddled the nut over it. He had to make a spanner to do it up or rather he got the blacksmith to make him a suitable spanner and he got it on tight. Behind that was a copper washer, which engaged the threads and was jammed into them, then you banged one corner of it up against the nut so it wouldn't come loose. There it was; the hands were on and the clock was ready to go. True, the hour hand was a bit grubby and elderly and the minute hand was beautifully new and gilded and straight. So he sent one of the several small boys to go and wind up the clock which of course ran on weight, a pendulum. He set the hands to midday and as the shadows reached their shortest point a small boy on the ground shouted, "Now!"

Whereupon he shouted at the boy inside the tower, "Let go of the pendulum!" and the clock started 'tick-tock, tick-tock.' When he came back 24 hours later it was a good five minutes slow, but he knew how to alter the timing of pendulum clocks. If you want it to go a bit faster, you shorten the pendulum. Well, actually you don't; you raise the centre of gravity of the pendulum weight and he did this by putting some more weights on top of it. Actually five minutes a day for a clock of that size he only had to add the equivalent of two copper coins on top of the pendulum. He ran it for another day and it was just about bang on. So he climbed down, took all the ladders away, undid the ropes and said to the verger, "I've finished. I'd now like to be paid."

The verger said "Arrr."

The clocksmith said, "What's the problem?"

"You'll have to give a bill in writing or the chapter won't pay you."

Very few people in Salisbury could write, but this young clocksmith could write extremely well so he said "Bill in writing? No trouble at all." So he went and bought a nice sheet of vellum and started lining it. He put: "For ye repair of ye great clock" and listed various items including: one bar of copper ten feet long (which I think was quite expensive) ten shillings, gilding 30 shillings, to making the nut (which the blacksmith had done) ten shillings, to the labour of doing so at a shilling a day for 6 days, 6 shillings, to ye great danger of climbing ladders (for which the hire of had also gone on the bill) 5 shillings and at the bottom he put: "to knowing how 6 guineas."

He then handed the bill to the verger who could read a bit because he'd been practicing on the Bible. He looked at it and said, "Look 'ere, you've charged for your danger money. You've charged for your labour and the hire of small boys, ropes, ladders and all that. You've charged for the materials. How can you possibly charge for knowing how on top of all that?"

"Well," said the clocksmith, "I doubt if anybody in Salisbury could do it and I came a long way from London knowing how to do it. Why don't you just take that up to the chapter? The fact is if they don't pay I'll take down the new hand and the nut. Yes I'll be slightly out of pocket on those two but I'll take them away. You'll be back where you were and you'll have egg all over your face. The town have seen me repairing the thing and getting it to keep accurate time over the last week. If the chapter don't choose to pay, they'll have egg all over their face as well."

"Arrr," said the verger and trotted into the chapter house where the chapter were sitting as it was a Wednesday. The verger explained the situation and they paid. No arguments at all! To knowing how is worth some money.

The History of Gentleman's Relish

Arthur Wesley was born in Ireland. There was a hymn singer of the same name and he felt it was a bit naff being called after a Holy Joe so he changed his name to Wellesley and then he went off to be a soldier. He could read, which was very surprising for soldiers of those days, and he went off to India with two huge crates of books. By the time he arrived in India by sailing ship, which took some time in those days because the bloody Frenchman hadn't dug the Suez Canal yet and he had to go round the Cape of Good Hope, he could already speak Hindustani with rather strange pronunciation and he knew the history of India and how to deal with the natives, which was very important.

He went there, fought several battles and won them all. I don't know if you read Bernard Cornwell books, but that Jack Savage character probably saved his life several times. I don't know whether it's true or not. Finally in 1805 they summoned him to go back to England and sent him next to Portugal where he had a bit of difficulty because, although he'd beaten the French quite easily, he was the only General there under 70. Well, he wasn't actually a full General but he was getting on - he was a Major General - his superior went and signed a thing called the Convention of Cintra, which enabled all the French to be sent home with their weapons in British warships. Luckily Wellesley refused to sign the Convention of Cintra much to the fury of the other aged Generals, who thought they'd done rather well.

When this convention, a copy of it, arrived in Parliament they were extremely angry because clearly the British army had defeated the French and they tried to take Wellesley to task for signing it. He said, "I never signed it. I disapproved of it strongly." Luckily his brother was the Earl of Mornington who had a great deal of influence. Anyway, everybody complained that he was only a Sepoy General, but he had beaten the French, who at the time had the best army in Europe. After a while he ended up as the only British general in Portugal, which he was trying to defend from the French who had invaded Spain and wanted all Europe. Bonaparte was behaving his usual way and made his brother Joseph King of Spain, which I don't think the Spaniards were too happy about.

However, the British army was rather small; there only was one and in fact Sir John Moore had done frightfully well getting it away from Corunna - he got shot doing it, but there it was. The establishment was very small and Arthur Wellesley hadn't got enough ADC's, so he sent a message out to all his relations in Ireland saying, "If you have a spare young son and he's got a good horse and a thick overcoat and enough money to live through the first winter, I'll probably be able to get him a proper job on the staff later on, but it makes a start in the profession, so come along." Come along they did. He had about twenty of these fellows. He behaved in the most unreliable way; he liked knowing what was going on on the other side of the hill, whereas the more senior Generals said that the spying was absolutely un-gentlemanly. At any rate, Wellesley had all these young men galloping about looking for him, but unfortunately the war office was very slow about giving him any increase in establishment. So these young men had run out of the twenty guineas they'd brought. But mind you, that went a long way in Portugal because the Maravedi, a very small Portuguese coin, were about four to the farthing and you could buy half a loaf of bread for a Maravedi. But eventually even that ran out and the only thing they could get reliably was ship's biscuit, which was pretty hard. They were designed to last; a ship's biscuit could be nailed down and used as flooring and that sort of thing and the only thing that can eat it is a weevil.

Nevertheless, Wellesley had a good relationship with the British Navy and they were able to keep even his unpaid young men supplied with ship's biscuit. What they used to do was go down to the seashore and buy a few sardines, cod or something like that, to pad out their ship's biscuit. One day they went down to the seashore, it must have been just after the equinoctial gales, which were about the middle of

September, and there were no ships at all. They had all been hauled up the beach, which was mainly black boulders, and stuck on top of the houses because an upside down boat with some ropes on it and boulders on the end of the ropes did keep the thatch on nicely at the equinoctial gales. They did find one chap whose boat wasn't up on the roof because he was mending a stove in plank. He was called Pedro the fisherman and he was famous for always laughing or singing or whistling or jollification - god knows why, he lived on a heap of bare rocks.

"Pedro," they said, "aren't you fishing?"

"No Señor," he said, "no es possible." Well, actually that's the wrong language but in Portuguese he said, "No, can't be done, it's the wrong time of year." When they used to go fishing they went out at night with nets and a lantern. The theory was it brought fish to the surface and they had a huge dog, it was a sort of poodle, a fishing poodle. If you said, "Show me the way to go home," it would turn its head towards home and bark so even in thick fog you could get home. So every fishing boat had two or three chaps in it to row it and man it, some nets, this great big dog and a lantern. The lantern of course was fed on olive oil because petroleum, fortunately, wasn't available.

So there was this band of hungry young men - Wellesley's Gallopers - looking at this boat and saying, "Pedro is there no chance of any fish?"

"Nothing," said Pedro, "de nada."

So they said, "Look Pedro, there's some interesting stuff that when this boat was upright must have got trodden into the bilges by mistake. There's a mixture of sardines, anchovies and a little bit of olive oil and don't of course forget the influence of the dog."

"And so what?" said Pedro.

So they said, "Could we scrape it out with the point of our penknives, between the cracks of the planking and spread it on our ship's biscuit to make it less unpalatable?"

"Oh, all right," said Pedro who was a very jolly chap. Pedro the fisherman was always singing (there's a song called that anyway) so they managed.

Eventually (I must shorten this story a bit) they got jobs in the establishment and they ended up in all sorts of important positions. One of them, a young chap called Somerset, eventually became the Earl of Raglan and damn nearly lost the Crimean war, but that was many years later. But they were jolly good as young Gallopers and more or less intelligence agents - because they used to gallop over the hills to see where the French were and got shot at a few times. They galloped back and said, "We've found where they are," which was very helpful. But eventually the Duke of Wellington died, which was about 1852 as far as I remember (but that's another story). It was raining and the Queen had just had the Crystal Palace exhibition opened especially for her the day before the public went in. Now by that time Arthur Wellesley was the Duke of Wellington. When the Queen sent for him he naturally obliged at once. He put on court dress, which was tight black breeches with white silk stockings and a cut-away coat, all that sort of thing, and you carried a top hat but of course you couldn't wear it in the presence of a monarch. It was 'lese majeste' to close a carriage if you were being rained on, because you might have been a Fenian with a bomb.

So he drove from No 1, London, which was at the corner of Hyde Park, up to where the Crystal Palace was and there was the Queen. Unfortunately, the Duke of Devonshire's gardener, who was later knighted for his efforts, enclosed a dozen or so lime trees within this huge exhibition hall, which had the very latest things in British steam engines and things all made of iron and brass, highly painted and polished and brilliantly displayed. Sir Henry Maudsley has just invented this lather and was saying how clever he was. Anyway, it was a great triumph of British engineering, and the Queen's hat (by the way hats were large that year) was black Italian straw and had been bombed by a sparrow. She said (you know she had a very strong accent), "Mine dear Duke, vat shal ve do? Look vat the sparrow has done to my hat."

He replied, "Ma'am have you tried sparrow hawks? And a very good day to you." He went home and caught pneumonia and died of a stroke six months later; very bad luck. But this is a diversion from the main bit of the story because that actually happened.

All of these young Gallopers ended up in positions of vast respectability like the Earl of Raglan and they all went to the Athenaeum. They used to sit around toasting their feet in the members' reading room, where anyone who was seen holding the Times more than three days old was carried out by the porters because he'd probably been dead for two or three days. The other ones toasted their feet and called for another glass of port. They toasted those fine jolly old days in the Peninsula (it was about 1808) and said, "You remember that delicious stuff we used to scrape out of the boats and put on our ship's biscuit?"

"Oh," they said, "gosh it was good. There's a new shop opened in town run by two gentleman. One is Mr Fortnum and the other is Mr Mason and they believe they're partners. Let's see if they can make something similar." So they went and explained the ingredients to Mr Fortnum and Mr Mason, who then produced something very like it but he was a bit at a loss as to what to do about the dog. But the anchovies and sardines and everything were stirred into a paste, with a certain amount of dried Atlantic Spray, and sold in little porcelain pots. Nowadays I think they're plastic but it tastes jolly good, especially on biscuits or hot buttered toast.

Anyway that's how gentleman's relish was invented, which of course has a Latin name - *Patum Peperium* - which means peppery paste. It was very peppery but had to have some to overcome the stale sardines.

Norman Words Creep Into English

When the Normans had conquered England they didn't feel very safe because of course they had stolen all the Saxons' land, who were a bit shirty about it. So after a while they took to building castles in a system known as motte and bailey. Now you think a motte is a moat don't you? Well, you're quite wrong; it's a big heap of earth. It was easy if you had lots of Saxons who were more or less slaves - serfs, bondsmen, lackeys, that sort of thing - you got them all out with baskets and some sort of digging implement. A spade in those days was made of wood as steel was reserved for weapons. You produced a huge heap of earth, stamped it down hard and on top of it you built a wooden thing like a castle. At least you could sleep there at night because the heap of earth was so steep that if you were attacking straight up it you'd probably skid if it was raining, which it often was. The bailey was another sort of wooden enclosure so that you had somewhere to keep your horses and things; sometimes they put up sheds in the bailey. Eventually, when castles became made of stone, there were a lot of sheds in the baileys, some of them fortified.

Anyway, in about 1250 the Normans starting building castles in stone. They brought a whole lot of very good stonemasons over from northern France who'd been set to work on cathedrals, but the pay wasn't very good. You know what Norman barons were like, always squabbling and trying to outbid the other for magnificence or something, so the one who had the most cash money at the time usually got the builders. Eventually castles were built of stone and they had a moat round them. The people who lived in these sort of things had to get on with the natives, the Saxons, so the windows especially down near the ground floor are very narrow, just arrow slits, because if you had anything any wider the Saxons would have swarmed in after dark and stolen the silver.

Now the system of dining was you started cooking about 4 o'clock in the afternoon. You had a great big fire in the kitchen - an open fronted fire - with several spits across it and depending how many people you expected to dinner you might have roasted an ox across it or it might have been something smaller like a hare. You couldn't just have one course for dinner; you had to have the odd goose and the occasional partridge and a few other things. In those days, believe it or not, they also ate vegetables. There were several vegetables available that had been introduced by the Romans. One of the most recent introductions of vegetables was broccoli, which actually came from Italy, funnily enough. I don't know why. Everybody knows that Brussels sprouts came from Brussels and they weren't very popular being difficult to boil. Broccoli was all right until the flowers opened and it turned yellow. Now, before the crusades, people kept straw on the floor and if there was anything they didn't want to eat they flung it over their shoulders and it got lost in the straw. If it was vegetables it stayed there and rotted, which is why they had to change the straw every year. But if it were anything edible, like a chicken bone or something, the dogs would eat it before it hit the straw. After the crusades, people got terribly civilised and started putting carpets on the floor, which meant you couldn't wear your spurs indoors. You had lackeys or chamberlains or something at the door saying, "Excuse me Sir, if you're coming to dinner would you mind taking off your spurs?" That was all right; you left your spurs and your sword and other things.

Dinner was usually served around dusk. My family always had jolly good candles because we used to go and rob the nearest church which had good, fat, wax candles made of beeswax, which were terribly expensive which is why the church could afford them and no one else could. Everybody else had things called tallow dips, which were terrible things; the wick was a piece of rush dipped into melted beef fat, several coats that were left to harden in between. Later on they were called penny dips or rush lights. They gave an awful, poor light and a terrible smell, but luckily we could always find a church to rob. The custom of dining was that the nobs always sat at a table across the hall and then down the length of the hall was a table of slightly lower level because the top table was on a dais, raised up a bit. All the workers and everybody else sat along this other, longer table and probably didn't get quite as smart food as the people at the top table. At the far end of the hall was a great big screen to try and keep the draught out. Sometimes it was a plain wooden screen, sometimes it was elaborately carved. The other side of the screen were a couple of serving tables and beyond that was the kitchen.

Now the kitchen had to be on the ground floor because you had all the rubbish to throw out and where else was there to throw it except into the moat? The rubbish mustn't be too big; it had to get through an arrow slit. So as it got dark, which was the main time for eating dinner, gradually the fire in the kitchen, which had been very bright, would burn down because they'd done all the important cooking. It got darker and darker, except at his lordship's table at the top where there were usually a couple of good, fat church candles burning. Sometimes if you didn't get caught too quickly you even got a candleholder with them as well; the best ones are silver and came out of churches of course.

Anyway, the two serving tables were of great importance because there were lots of young boys, who were going to be pages when they got a bit more civilised and were scrubbed a few times. But to start with they were called leashers because their job was to lick the plates clean between courses. Running water hadn't as yet been invented, well it had been by the Romans but the British had gone backwards since then. So if you were in a stone castle around six o'clock in the evening in February when it was pitch dark the leashers had to remove the plates from the previous course. Perhaps I forgot to explain, you couldn't throw things over your shoulder anymore because it would ruin the carpet. So you put the bits you didn't want to eat back on your plate, these included things like chicken bones and the butt end of asparagus where it got too stringy to eat and broccoli where the flowers had already opened and were showing bright yellow - one didn't have to eat that sort of thing - artichoke leaves and all the gubbins, cabbage stalks and all that.

Anyway, the leashers would take your plates away and the next course would be brought. His Lordship would be up at the top table and there was often a pause between the removes, as they called them, when you probably had six different courses of meat to start with and then finally, meat was over, it was obviously going to be pudding. So the leashers had to get the plates really quite clean and his lordship sat there saying, "Where's the bloody pudding?" and banging his pewter pot on the table. Now they had tried glass glasses like the Romans, but they broke too easily, so they'd gone back to pewter, which was quite sensible really. His Lordship would be demanding his pudding and the head butler, major domo or whatever you called him, would be hissing at the leashers, "Hurry up, his Lordship wants his pudding!" Depending on how they were getting on in the kitchen sometimes there was an awful delay and it was terribly dark behind the screen where these two serving tables were.

Now I'll digress slightly because there were many Norman words, which had crept into the English language. There was of course ullage, boskage and sockage. Every schoolboy knows what they are, surely? Although, they've stopped teaching anything useful in school. Ullage was the right to the lees of wine, the sort of sludgy bits at the bottom of the cask. Sockage was the right to eat any meat that was left over from the high table. Boskage was the right to pick up only dead twigs; you mustn't cut any live twigs in his Lordship's woods and hunting preserves and so on. You had to have a few sticks to cook your meals on, so that was allowed. There were all the various things you owed the crown, like homage. Homage was from homme meaning men. You promised to turn out for the crown when called upon a certain number of armed men. There was scutage, which was a tax on shields, because you had to find some taxes somewhere, and there were many other good Norman words. You've often heard the town crier saying, "Oyez, oyez," haven't you? This was another Norman word meaning listen. I don't know if they did listen because they were Saxons and bolshy. There was another fine Norman word, curfew which is a corruption of couvre feu, cover your fires, because everything was made of wood in those days and if you went to sleep and left your fire burning you'd probably burn the whole town down. So by law you had to cover your fire with ashes at a given hour and the hour of curfew or 'couvre feu' was known because somebody rang a bell and that was the curfew hour.

However, to get back to the dining customs, just occasionally they'd make a slight mistake and when his Lordship was in a terrible bad temper - say he'd been hunting all afternoon and hadn't got anything and he had some terribly important guests to dinner and they had to eat yesterday's cold, boiled beef which is enough to put anybody into a bad temper - and he'd bang the table with his pint pot and say, "Where's my pudding?" and the major domo or butler whatever you called him would say to the leashers, "Now hurry up, bring in the plates at once." Every now and then they'd make a mistake and they'd bring back a plate covered in old artichoke leaves, broccoli that had turned yellow, cabbage stalks and that sort of thing. When that was plonked down at the high table in front of his Lordship or his guests, all his guests thought it was a frightful funny joke and they would point their fingers at his Lordship and say, "Vomage! Hahaha! Teeheehee."

The First Settlers in South Africa

Many hundreds of years ago an Irishman called Padraig Murphy had been up in the bogs cutting turf to make peats, which he stacked in the correct herringbone fashion so they would dry out and make good winter fuel. During this he developed a terrible thirst. So he went down to the nearest place he thought he could get a sop or something. The kind of thirst he had wasn't one that could be cured with water; there was plenty of water everywhere. He went down to the nearest place, which was a small port called Dun Laoghaire. Where he'd been up in the bog he hadn't heard the church bells and so he hadn't realised it was a Sunday. When he got down there everything was shut and it was starting to get dark and he had this terrible thirst on him. He noticed there was a ship in port and he didn't see anybody there so he crept on board. The deck was covered in barrels. "Now," he thought, "that's fine, they'll give me a job unloading them tomorrow and I'll get a decent sop which might cure me thirst." Well, he was pretty tired and it had got dark so he hid himself between these barrels, lay down and actually went to sleep. As you've probably realised, Padraig Murphy wasn't the sharpest knife in the box. When he awoke again the ship was at sea, there was no land in sight and as far as he could tell they were headed south.

He knew the further south you went the hotter it got. At any rate as he was starving and really quite thirsty he made himself known to the crew who were a funny lot. The only language he spoke was Eirse and the only language these people spoke was double Dutch, which he wasn't used to so they couldn't really converse at all except with hand signals. When he pointed out he was hungry and thirsty they fed him with some ordinary sort of seafaring stuff, salt pork or something and I suppose they made chapattis out of something or other.

Anyway he got on all right and they found him somewhere to sleep inside the ship instead of on the deck. There were some livestock on board so they made him muck them out and feed them and look after them. I don't know how many – horses, a few cows and some sheep – not an awful lot, but it kept him quite busy. The further south they went, the hotter it got and then suddenly greatly to his surprise he found it was getting colder again. "Well," he thought, "this is crazy. The world must have turned upside down. Surely the further south you go the hotter it gets." Not in this case though. It got colder and colder and colder. By the time it was the end of June it'd got really quite nippy and rather stormy; it was a bit terrifying.

In July they put into a place which wasn't much of a harbour really, and it had this funny flat-topped mountain behind it. It was a bit foggy and it tended to rain a lot. He didn't like the look of it at all, but these double Dutchies all wore the most extraordinary clothes. They had black breeches, black stockings, a white shirt, black waistcoat and a long black thick woollen cloak and a great big black steeple hat and of course buckled shoes. He had only the clothes he stood up in, which were designed for April in Ireland, and he found it was damned chilly. They got him to push the barrels over board, which is always terrible, and then some people in a rowing boat chivvied them so they floated into the beach. Then they got Padraig down there to push the barrels up the beach above the high tide mark. They got him working; he was rather able to work, a big strong fellow. They unloaded a cart with the wheels off and so on and the draw bar was separate. They got all that onto a rowing boat and rowed it ashore. They didn't fancy putting livestock in the boat so they just loaded them over the side and made them swim for it, which they were all able to do. Padraig was told to round them up, using all these signs and gestures as he didn't understand a word of their double Dutch. Then the carts were put together and a couple of horses were harnessed to it and they put some of these barrels on it – only some as there were quite a lot.

They gave Padraig a spade and took him quite a way inland and started making him dig little trenches. Not very big, only about a foot deep and a hundred yards long, several trenches all parallel to each other about six feet apart. Then they opened one of these barrels and he was terribly disappointed because they contained damp sawdust with some little twigs in them. He thought, "Now what?"

The twigs were actually vine cuttings and when you have a vine cutting and you plant it the wrong way up it doesn't grow. It only grows if you plant it the right way up. These double Dutchies must have been quite cunning because the vine cuttings had a pointed end at the top and a square cut end at the bottom. He was told to plant them all with the square cut end down, so he did that. There were hundreds of thousands of these things; they kept him busy for quite some time.

In the meantime the double Dutchies, who took their hats and cloaks off when they were working, started quarrying stone at the foot of this mountain. They'd already flung up a few mud huts from sticks and mud and wattle that everyone was living in. Padraig had already built himself a thing, which really frankly was no better than a pigsty but it was useable. In the meantime with these quarried stones they built very carefully. They made huge trenches and level foundations and pounded rock into the bottom. Then they found some limestone and put up a lime kiln, found enough firewood and were busy burning lime because cement wasn't readily available (after all it was made in a factory in Rugby that wasn't to be built for 300 years). They built this splendid great building and Padraig thought, "If only it had a steeple it'd be a church," but there was no steeple. It had some narrow windows in it, which they shut with shutters to keep the draught out and they put in a whole lot of benches. It was obviously going to be a meeting house of some sort. Practically every evening they were in there and wouldn't let Padraig in. He was quite miserable outside and there wasn't a lot to eat. However, they had tilled some land and started growing some crops. Padraig could plough; he'd run two horses at the plough, which made him quite useful. But the crops hadn't come up yet and they were still living on rather scant provisions from the ship.

Anyway, they built this big solid building and built it very well, too. They roofed it properly with thin slates made from split rock and great big timber beams to hold the whole thing up. It was a thoroughly smart thing, but they wouldn't let him in. It had a watchman on the door, who was rather short sighted, and he'd let everyone in except Padraig Murphy. When the watchman saw Padraig, he waved him away because they couldn't talk to each other. Padraig was beginning to understand a little bit and he learnt that the chief one of these people – they were all called Van something or other – was called Van Riebeeck. He learnt from listening to the people going into this warm meeting house, which was nice and snug when it had a couple of hundred people in it and the windows and doors were shut (how he longed to be in there in the evenings).

One day he was prowling round the town to see if there was anything new, or frankly if there was anything spare to eat or drink, when he found one of these old Van's dropped dead in the street. Nobody in sight so he thought, "Goodness, I can get myself some warm clothes," and he soon did. He stripped the fellow off and put his clothes on and Padraig's old clothes on the corpse, which was lying in the street. No signs of injury or anything, probably old age or heart attack had knocked him down. Then he went up to the meeting house as it had just got dark and people were still going in. The rather shortsighted chap on the door said to him, "Vas de nom?" and he said, "Van de Murphy." They let him in and he's been there ever since.

Sodium Sulphate

In the late 17th century there was a Herr Doctor Glauber who ran a spa in Northern Germany where there are many hot springs. He had some very sulphurous water, which contained a thing called Glauber's salt as it was named after the Herr Doctor Glauber. It is in fact sodium sulphate. Epsom salt is magnesium sulphate and sodium sulphate has the same effect; it turns you inside out. The spa was probably at a place called Bad something, as bad is the German for bath. I'd like to suggest it should have been called Bad Schmelling because of these sulphurous fumes everywhere.

Now he wanted to drum up business and in the 1680s the Hanoverian royal family had not been offered the crown of England, which they were later, but they still looked very humpty dumpty shaped and he thought he could fix this. So he told them, "Come and stay at my spa. You'll find it cheaper than staying at home. I'll give you a fortnight at my spa with 20% off so long as you all come." (There were about half a dozen of them). Now the thing about the Hanoverians was they had the most beautiful horses. They were absolutely lovely, but they themselves and their mistresses were extremely plain; of the two I would have chosen the horses.

Nevertheless they trekked off to this spa. He was very meticulous, Herr Doctor Glauber. He weighed them and measured them before they started and weighed and measured them when they went. While they were there he reduced them from six meals a day to three, from eight courses per meal to four with much smaller portions and he made them drink two pints of this filthy pump water. The interesting thing was when they went away they weighed and measured exactly the same as when they arrived and he made a most perceptive remark considering the age in which it was said. He said, "Perhaps it's hereditary."

Mustard

In the middle of the 18th century Parson Colman, who had inherited two water mills both of which were listed in the Doomsday Book, had a terrible commercial shock. He grew saffron and indigo. Unfortunately the saffron, which is the stamens of the autumn crocus and gives you terrible backache picking, had been outdated by safflower oil coming from India. Indigo had been replaced by ammonium thiosulphate, which of course was Prussian blue invented by some Prussian chemist.

These innovations gave Parson Colman a terrible shock as his income had ceased and he was a parson on a rather poor living, without a high population. Worse, he had just bought, on credit, a brand new pair of Mantons – beautiful shotguns, the best available as he was very fond of partridge shooting. Well, he had several sons. One of them went off into the army, another into the navy and no doubt one went into banking or something, but his youngest son said, "Daddy, I want to be a parson."

He said, "Come off it son. There's no money in it at all. You'll never make a living at it."

"Oh, but Daddy I would very much like to go and see the holy land." He was absolutely determined so his father borrowed enough shillings and pounds and got him across the channel. England was not at war with France at the time, very fortunately. Eventually he got down into Northern Italy and took a boat, probably from Venice, to go to the holy land. The Venetians had the monopoly of trade in the Eastern Mediterranean and dealt particularly with things like silks and spices.

Anyway, after a few excursions and dodging about to miss the Barbary pirates and all that, they arrived in the holy land. A gully gully man came up and made the usual sort of obscene suggestions. "No," he said. "I don't want to see any of those. I want to see the Stations of the oss and the Mount of Olives." I suppose when he got to the Mount of Olives he found it was already a housing estate, but I don't know. I wasn't there at the time. The gully gully man was quite helpful, really. He was paying him half a piastre a day, which is quite a lot for a gully gully man. He said, "I want to see the mustard tree which bringeth forth an hundredfold."

The gully gully man couldn't make head or tail of that so he said, "Look around at all these fields. They're yellow, that's mustard."

"Oh, but I thought it grew right under the sun in furthest Arabia and that's why it's so hot."

"No," the gully gully man said, "it grows here," and he explained what they did with it. "First of all you put it between the stones of a mill, which are not quite touching. That cracks the seed coat of the mustard." The seed is very small; it looks like a cabbage seed and is grey. When you crack the seed coat and you winnow it and the wind blows the seed coat away, you're left with these little yellow seeds with no coat. "Then," the gully gully man said, "you fill a leather bag with the seed, sew it up tightly and then put it under a screw press." The screw presses of those days had a wooden screw thread and the threads were probably two to the inch maximum. By twisting the ends of this, you could put some very considerable pressure on anything underneath it. So they would squash the bag. The leather was sufficiently porous to let the mustard oil out where it was caught in a large tray, bottled and used for cooking. They cooked their chapattis or whatever they had in mustard oil; it was a local habit. Nowadays we use rapeseed oil, which is similar. Then they emptied the leather bag, which was full of yellow sludge, far too hot to eat, so they dried it and sold it to the Venetians, who took it away and told lies about its origin. They said it came from directly under the sun on the far side of Arabia and they sold it to people in Europe to put on their rather dull salt meat. You had to kill most of your animals at Michaelmas and salt them down in barrels because there wasn't enough hay to keep them all through winter.

Young Colman said to the gully gully man, "Can you get me a pound of seed?"

The man said, "A pound? I can get you a 150 pound bag quite easily, but to get one pound we're going to have to break bulk and the shop keepers here will be awfully cross. They sell mustard oil; they don't want to sell individual bags of mustard seed." At any rate, after a lot of arguments and hassle he was able to get a pound of mustard seed, which he put in his pocket. In those days people were dressed exactly like one of those old fashioned pictures of Gulliver and he had an overcoat with turned back sleeves and all those sorts of things, but most importantly big pockets. He poured the seed into his pocket. Unfortunately, there was a hole in the pocket and the seed eventually worked its way through into the lining.

When he got home his nanny appeared and said, "Oh dear, your stockings have fallen down again. Why don't you do up your garters? Your coat's in a disgusting state. I'll take it away and wash it. Now take it off immediately! Oh, and look the lining is full of rubbish. I'll take that out and burn it."

"No!" he said. "Don't do that. Those seeds are for Dad and the minute he comes back from evening sermon I'll give him the seeds. So you sort that out." So she separated the fluff from the seeds and eventually produced more or less a pound of mustard seed. When his dad appeared, he was really quite pleased to see him back again because some of his sons had gone away and never come back. The boy said, "Dad, I've got the answer to your partridge shooting. I went to the holy land and I asked for the mustard tree which bringeth forth an hundredfold and they showed me fields of it. They were full of quail and partridge and all sorts of edible game birds. They don't seem to have pheasants there though."

Parson Coleman said, "Well that's very interesting." He planted the pound of mustard seeds, which of course rapidly became a hundred pounds and with that he was able to plant two acres and in no time he had four hundred acres worth. One of his water mills was back in work decorticating the mustard seed and he soon got a cunning artificer in Norwich to make him a screw press and he pressed out the oil. I don't know how well it sold in England for cooking oil, as most people in those days cooked in either lard or butter. However, he regarded the oil as a waste product. It was the yellow sludge left in the middle he was interested in. So having dried it, he packed it into little square tins marked Colman's, Norwich Mustard. The labels were yellow and they still are today. He made such a profit that in no time at all, maybe two or three years, he was able to pay for his Mantons, which were the most expensive and delightful guns you could buy in those days. His partridge shooting was greatly improved as they loved living at the bottom of the mustard plants and so they all lived happily ever after.

Boston's Tea Party

Poor old George the Third had a bad go of porphyria and was mad most of the time, but he had an excellent prime minister called William Pitt who managed the country's business quite well until he died, unfortunately, quite young. However, there were thirteen quite useless colonies in America because they didn't pay enough taxes to justify themselves and they were rather bolshy and spoke English. There was a tax on tea. Tea was quite an expensive commodity in those days; a pound would have cost a guinea. The tax to the king was probably two shillings. So it was an expensive thing. The American colonies had started realising that they were being had for a mug by the British as they had to pay taxes but had absolutely no representation in parliament.

So they thought what can we do and first of all they took to brewing untaxed liquor up in the hills, moonshine. That cut off some of the king's revenue. They said, "This is much better than tea and it isn't taxed," so they weren't buying very much tea from all the merchants in Boston, who were considerably rich. All their go-downs were absolutely stuffed with tea, which in those days came from China. As you probably realise, they hadn't grown tea in India yet, although there was a little bit starting in Ceylon. So what actually happened was Pitt went to see King George who was suddenly sane one day – he had these little patches of sanity – and said, "The colonists are complaining."

And the King asked, "What are they complaining about?"
Pitt said, "The taxes on tea."
"Oh yes," said George. "What does it bring in?"
"£20,000 a year."
"Really?" said the king. "And what does the household cavalry cost me?"

"£22,000 a year"

"Oh, well scrap the tax on tea." He was a very reasonable chap when he was sane. So this message - it only took about three months to cross the Atlantic - that they'd scrapped the tax on tea arrived. It was no good by then; the colonists were firmly stuck into their Kentucky moonshine and so these warehouses remained bulging full of tea, which wasn't selling. Then a tea clipper arrived from China - actually it was one of those well-built, pine, fast clippers. Most Britons think the clipper was a British thing. It wasn't. It was an American thing and they were much faster than any British ship. The East Indiamen carried hundreds of tons of cargo but were quite slow. A clipper was quite important; it helped get the first cargo of the season back first so you received a good price for it. Anyway, a clipper appeared in Boston harbour whereupon the merchants all, well, they took off their wigs for a start and scratched the stubble underneath because a lot of them had nits in those days. They said, "What shall we do about this?" They decided what to do and they got all their warehousemen to dress up as Red Indians that night. Luckily it was quite a warm night as they were more or less shirtless, and they ran around with tomahawks and threw all the tea in the harbour. Now a lot of people think that this was an American blow for independence. It wasn't. It was the merchants trying to look after their profits.

Worcestershire Sauce

Many years ago there was a South Sea bubble and even after it had collapsed people had become faintly interested in the strange new products coming from places that had been discovered by, for instance, Captain Cook. Now there was a grocer called Mr Lea in Worcester who had an assistant called Mr Perrins, the one who did all the work and stacked the shelves. He was always being badgered by salesmen saying, "Oh, you should have some of this. You should have some of that. It's the latest from the South Seas." They offered him mangoes and chillies and they said, "Of course, you'll get all the carriage trade if you have all these smart new things. They'll have read about them." He wasn't entirely convinced but he bought a box of each, although the mangoes came in big bamboo baskets so you had to buy quite a lot. They sat on the shelves and the carriage trade weren't interested as they'd never heard of them and weren't going to eat something they weren't used to.

So a whole lot of these foreign things sat on the shelves until they began to wilt, whereupon his assistant, Mr Perrins, said, "You can't have the shop looking like this with things half rotten all over the shelves." So he flung them in a barrel in the back yard. It was an open-topped barrel and it had a certain amount of rainwater in it. He put all sorts of thing in there, including all the new stuff from the South Seas (or thereabouts as the fact is some of them actually came from India and places like that). After a year or two the salesmen stopped calling as he wasn't going to buy any more. The contents of the barrel rotted down and, as it was an open-topped barrel, in the summer a bit of the water would evaporate and in the winter it'd top it up again, and of course it was open to all the coal smoke in Worcester.

After about two or three years Perrins thought, "That's funny, this smells rather nice." He stuck his finger in the barrel and licked it and thought, "Well that's rather surprising." So he sent for Mr Lea. "Excuse me sir," he said, "but that stuff we threw into the barrel has turned into quite a nice tasting mixture. It's a bit sharp, but I wonder if we couldn't do something with it? Maybe bottling it and selling it as a sauce?"

So Mr Lea stuck his finger into it and tasted it and said, "That's an idea. I think that would be jolly good on mince and perhaps on toasted cheese and one or two other things." So they bottled it, sold it and they did very well out of it. They didn't make a fortune, but they did very well indeed. They could more or less give up the shop and just stick to making this mixture. So Mr Perrins was made a partner and you can still buy this stuff to this very day. It's called Worcestershire Sauce.

The First Battle of Copenhagen

Of course it was not the first battle of Copenhagen; they had probably been having skirmishes there for hundreds of years, if not thousands, but it was the first battle at Copenhagen where the British were involved. Everybody remembered it because Nelson was there, who was a very successful sailor and well-known naval hero. He'd been sent there and at this battle, or just before it I should say, Nelson made a really famous remark, which holds as true today as when he said it. He was only vice-admiral to a fellow called Sir Hyde-Parker – extraordinary name and they didn't name the park after him either. Nelson was a parson's son, kept his fingernails clean and knew how to eat properly with good table manners.

Now the British were very worried about the Danish fleet, which was quite large. Napoleon was advancing by land and the British got there by sea. Nelson, because he had good table manners and such and probably could speak enough French to be understood, was sent on shore to go and negotiate with the Danes whose king was called Christian the Fourth (their kings are always called Christian so you have to remember which number). Now, the one on that particular day was Christian the Fourth – very nice chap, good table. He was a very decent chap with eight course dinners and different wine with every course and port and brandy afterwards. Although Nelson, in fact, was extremely abstemious and didn't get drunk as he had to keep his head about him because he was trying to negotiate.

The battle itself was on the second of April 1801. There had, as I say, been other battles and there was later a second battle of Copenhagen involving the British. But then this history is biased really in favour, or not in favour, of the British. It is about the British because, after all, we invented and wrote all the best history and history is always written by the winners, isn't it? Anyway Nelson went on shore and was given a splendid dinner every night by this dear nice, kind chap King Christian the Fourth, who explained, "Look, I really can't give you the fleet because Napoleon is coming by land and nobody can stop him on land and he'll burn the city, behave no how and things will be thoroughly tiresome. So although I don't want to give my fleet away to anybody, I'm afraid I'll have to. I daren't give it to you because we'll all get massacred by the French."

Then Nelson said, "Well, you do see the English problem don't you? The French have got quite a large fleet already and if they add the Danish fleet to it they'll then outnumber the British fleet totally. We are in a desperate position. We'll lose all our foreign trade and we'll go bust, have nothing to eat and all sorts of other terrible disabilities. Then the French will invade us and behave no how."

Revolutionary France lived entirely in a climate of fear. The secret police encouraged everybody to spy on everybody else and they were all frightened of being denounced. Any old scores were settled; you'd say so-and-so's plotting against the republic when actually you just owed him money and they'd whip him away and guillotine him. Very nice people they were, foreigners of course.

Anyway, Nelson had many good dinners, some people say as many as six, but at the end of it they couldn't agree. The British had to prevent the fleet falling into French hands and hopefully they said to King Christian the Fourth, "Why don't you come and join us? We'll feed you and pay you and you can be on our side and all will be well.

Poor old King Christian said, "You know, that's fine but can you stop Napoleon on land? The answer is no you can't." Nobody could at that particular time. So they agreed eventually to hold a battle on, I think it was the Saturday, as far as I can remember. The second of April was a Saturday, but I could be mistaken. They agreed to start firing when the clock, which was in a lovely copper topped tower (it turned green of course), struck the first stroke of twelve. You got the four quarter chimes, which gave you some warning so you could make sure your guns were pointing the right way. Now, of course, the British are noble, modest and honest and while the Danes had been doing a little cheating, the British had cheated even harder. The Danes had chained all their ships together and had cut extra gun ports in the side of their ships so that every gun on board could be facing the seaward side from which the British were expected to attack. Of course, a ship which is chained in a long row of ships can't manoeuvre in any way – that is just one disadvantage. The other thing was, as the Danish ships were all absolutely immovable and strung right across the mouth of the harbour, the shore batteries couldn't fire, as they'd have been firing into their own ships. That's cheating, but you want to hear what Nelson did! Every night while he was having dinner with the dear, kind, generous King Christian the Fourth he had rowing boats out with muffled oars. Now I don't know if you know how to muffle an oar, but the point is to stop it squeaking and such, so you wrap some old torn sailcloth round the shaft of the oar where it goes through the tholepins. The navy didn't use rowlocks, which are the metal things which pivot which you might get in a modern rowing boat. They just had stout timbers, two sticking up, and rested the oar between it in a sort of slot. The oar at that point was covered with leather to stop the tholepins chaffing through the wood and if you covered the whole lot with some old torn clothes or usually old sailcloth and wrapped it round a few times it didn't squeak and rattle. So provided you didn't catch a crab, when you rowed slowly you could go very, very silently. Of course the electric torch had not yet been invented so Nelson's rowing boats took soundings of the harbour right to the shore line and, to cut a long story much shorter, he discovered that the end Danish ship didn't quite block off the entire harbour. There was just room, only perhaps a couple of feet to spare, to get a seventy-four gun ship through, but you had to steer very straight and be absolutely sure of where you were going. As he was a great chap for holding conferences with all his captains, long before the day of the battle they all knew exactly what to do.

    I can't remember which ship Nelson was in, I think it might have been the *Agamemnon*, but as he was Vice-Admiral he didn't command the ship; he commanded the squadron and he had a flag captain, a fellow called Hardy who gave the orders to set the sails and do the things you do on ships. Nelson was a very bad sailor, as you know; he suffered terribly from sea sickness and it had taken them three weeks to get to Denmark and for the first fortnight he was as sick as a dog. Then he was very pleased to be on shore and get some proper food. On ships in those days the food wasn't terribly good, but at least you got fed every day and didn't starve; times were hard.

Because there was a battle about to be fought at twelve o'clock, well on the first stroke of twelve, Nelson was a bit tetchy. He knew he'd either be dead or sailing home again immediately afterwards and he was getting a bit irritable. The men had all been fed at eleven and then they had to put out all the fires on board. There was only one candle and that was kept well away from the magazine under a pot of Stockholm tar down in the cockpit. This was where the surgeon would scrape all the rust off his saws and was getting ready for the amputations. Nelson and other people didn't like that at all; it made him feel very queasy, but it was necessary. So there was this smell of Stockholm tar coming up and being the second of April, of course the harbour ice had melted. The Danes eat an awful lot of pickled herring. They're very fond of them and they had barrels and barrels of them, but when you pickle a herring in a barrel, of course you cut the head off and throw it into the nearest disposal place, which is the harbour. This is fine in the winter because it freezes over and they don't smell, but when the ice melts the seagulls get ecstatic with delight as all these rotten fish heads come to the surface along with any other stuff that's been thrown into the harbour.

Harbours have a bad reputation because, you know, the plumbing wasn't very good. But worse than this, when the admiral walks his quarterdeck, everybody else must keep down-wind of him. The theory is that the lower classes stink. The admiral probably did too, but he had the right to be up-wind. When you're walking across a quarterdeck back and forth, a seventy-four has got a fair beam, but nevertheless it's not a very long walk. He had a procession of people following him and of course the nearest one was his flag captain Hardy, who unfortunately, although he was a naval officer, tried to follow the latest fashions. Now I don't know if you remember, in 1801, Beau Brummel had persuaded the Prince Regent that cravats should be very high. Really this was because Beau was a sensible sort of fawning toady and the Prince Regent had about three or four double chins. High cravats definitely made him look a bit better, so with cravats it was fashionable to have them very, very high and Hardy was wearing a very high cravat. The naval uniform covered your hat, coat and breeches, but it didn't cover your shirt and cravat. You were meant to wear a plain coloured shirt, white usually, but unfortunately due to the sort of food you get at sea, which is salted this and dried that, he was developing a boil, possibly a carbuncle, on his neck. Anyway, just before noon Nelson was getting very tetchy and every time Hardy thought Nelson couldn't see him he'd take his hand up to his cravat to try and get a finger down the back of his neck to get at his carbuncle. Eventually Nelson made this remark, which is as true today as when he said it; it is a really very, very famous remark.

You can understand why Nelson was feeling a bit tetchy; the men had all got indigestion, the fires had been thrown overboard and he knew someone was going to get killed. He didn't actually enjoy battle, but he was determined to prosecute them as hard as he could for Britain's honour and glory. The interesting thing is the tactics were just about the same as they had been at the battle of the Nile, which he'd won previously, much to Napoleon's discomfiture, as they'd actually been fighting the French fleet. Well, what happened was they got inshore up the Nile of these anchored French ships and went up the line and destroyed practically the whole lot. I think only two got away. One of them, a huge ship, blew up because its magazine went up and there was flaming debris in all directions. I think that's what happened to Nelsons eye.

In the course of the first battle of Copenhagen one of the ships, I'm not sure which one, it could have been the *Hannibal*, actually went aground getting through this little, tiny, narrow gap to get inshore of the Danish ships, which were all chained together. Whereupon Sir Hyde-Parker sent up a signal saying withdraw. Well, it wasn't practical, actually, because several ships were beyond the one that had got aground and were already engaging the Danes and the ship was stuck there and you couldn't withdraw. Also Nelson was quite sure that he was going to win the battle; the only trouble was getting the ship that was aground off, but they managed it and it got through the gap and they went up the whole Danish line and they sank the lot, which may have upset the Danes a bit. I expect a lot of them were killed but there it was; they wouldn't do the right thing, which was to join the British fleet. But he made this very, very famous remark just before the battle started actually and it holds as true today as when he said it; "Hardy," he said, "it'll never get well if you pick it!"

Beef Wellington

When Arthur Wellesley was recalled from India he was ordered to go and run the very small army that the British had inserted into Portugal, as the French were invading the whole of Europe and Britain only had a very small army. It had been surrounded by the French and chased through the Portuguese mountains. It had got away at Corunna under the management of an excellent General called Sir John Moore, who had invented the Light Brigade. Unfortunately, he was killed during the evacuation, but he got the very small army away. The Royal Navy were very helpful there. They were sent back further south into Portugal, but they got a new General. He was a sickly old man with gout who sat in his coach all day and never did anything useful. He never knew where the French were as he couldn't go anywhere and couldn't ride a horse. He was the Head General, but they sent this young chap Arthur Wellesley to be his junior general; Wellesley had been so good with the sepoys in India. He'd fought dozens of battles and won them all because he kept his powder dry and knew how to organise people.

This fellow Wellesley sent messages to Ireland, as he came from there, and asked all his friends to send their spare younger sons out to be ADC's and he would get them on the establishment, whereupon he'd get them properly paid with uniforms, etc. All they had to do was bring a good horse, a thick overcoat and enough money to feed them through the winter. Most of them were quite successful when he got them on the establishment; they rose to be Major Generals. However, to all these young gallopers he said, "I will not have gallant officers. If you get within range of the French and they shoot you, you're of no use to me. I just want to know where the French are." Of course, the old

General thought this was absolutely terrible. He thought it was spying, not a gentlemanly profession at all.

At any rate, Wellesley prevailed as this old man was stuck in his coach all day and eventually Wellesley captured a good chunk of the French army by knowing where they were. This old General, whose name I'm not going to tell you, although I know it, as I don't wish to malign him, got the British Navy to take these French troops back to France, with all their weapons and full honours of war.

He'd signed a thing called the Convention of Cintra, which allowed the French to do this. Well, when this hit the British Parliament it was like a bomb. They said, "You can't behave like that. These are French revolutionaries and they use guillotines, are terrorists and behave no how. It should never have happened. Who's the fellow who signed it? Now, luckily, Wellesley's older brother was called Lord Mornington and he pointed out in the House of Lords to the rest of parliament that his younger brother had never signed it and didn't approve of it any more than parliament did. So the outcome was that the older General was never employed again; he took himself home with his gout and died. There was Wellesley, so they promoted him to Major General and put him in charge of the forces in Portugal.

Eventually he was able to get all these young men on his establishment. They were all made into some sort of officer. The trouble was they were all busy exploring the countryside and they started well before dawn so they'd get to the French at the time they were lighting their campfires. They could see where they were, what they were doing and whether they had they moved since yesterday. All this was plotted on maps back at Wellesley's headquarters, which gave him a very good idea of the direction they were moving in, whether they were massing for an assault or a siege. It enabled him to outwit them and to catch little segments of the French army or occasionally to catch large segments by surrounding them and cutting off their supplies until there was very little they could do.

However, all these gallopers or ADC's, spies some people called them, were very busy men and they rode like mad and often came back a bit late for lunch. So Wellington, or Wellesley as he called himself then, as he hadn't been made into the Duke of Wellington yet, was full of good ideas and had a notion of how to keep beef hot despite the fact a lot of his chaps ate very late for lunch. So he had fillets of beef rolled in pastry. You just cut a little slice off the end so you've got a bit of outside pastry with a bit of beef in the middle. If it was nice fluffy pastry, it's surprising how long it stayed hot. You could turn up for lunch at half past three and still get a reasonably hot bit of fillet. It's been called Beef Wellington to this day.

Good Advice When Visiting Foreign Parts

Lord Macaulay the Elder was sitting in his study reading some Thucydides in the original Greek because he didn't trust translations – he thought they might not be accurate – with his feet up on a gout stool and a bottle of port well within reach. Port bottles were smaller in those days; there really were three bottle men as they were only half a litre each. The butler disturbed his concentration by banging on the door. "All right," he said, "what is it?"

The butler said, "Mi'lord, they have repaired the coach. Your second son has returned from his grand tour of Europe and it is ready to take your third son on the grand tour of Europe."

"Jolly good," said Lord Macaulay, "now send him away and I'll get on with my Thucydides."

The butler sort of coughed a bit and said, "It is customary for your Lordship to give the young gentleman a few words of advice."

"Oh by golly, so it is, so it is. What's his name? What's his name? Send him in!"

"Thomas, my lord," (the one who later wrote all the biased anti-catholic history).

So this young gentleman was shown in who bowed and he always called his father Sir, which was quite correct and proper, and Lord Macaulay said, "Now listen," and Thomas said, "Sir?"

"Black men start at Calais, but you'll find that English will suffice provided you speak it more loudly, more slowly and more distinctly. There is no point in talking to Dutch men because they respond to no known language." The butler sort of shuffled and looked at the floor a bit and his Lordship said, "Ah yes, and another bit of advice. When in Rome do as at home. Sleep with your windows shut or you'll catch the fever." The butler sort of shuffled his feet and coughed a bit and looked at the floor. Macaulay remembered, "Oh yes, here's a bag of 500 guineas. If I were you I'd spend it on wine, women and song. Women are really most rewarding, wine gives you a headache and song can be awfully boring if it's Wagner or somebody like that." (Wagner hadn't been born for about a hundred years, but I doubt whether it will spoil the story). "You're not to buy the Elgin Marbles. It'll probably break the back axle of the coach. Now be off with you."

The Railway Bun

When Isambard Kingdom Brunel built the Great Western Railway a lot of people called it God's wonderful railway because he did build it quite differently to anybody else's railway. For a start, the sleepers ran longitudinally under the rails and were carried on piles driven deep down into the soil. The gauge between the rails, instead of being four foot eight and a half like Stevenson, who had copied it from the Roman grooves in the paving at York, Brunei made the gauge seven foot. This produced, or should have, a smoother ride and it was indeed a very wonderful railway.

When the Great Western Railway spread over huge parts of England it went eventually as far north as Crewe. Now Crewe is a junction of all sorts of railways: the Midland Railway, the North Western Railway, the Great Western Railway, the Cambrian Railway, the Cheshire Committee Lines and I expect the Lancashire and Yorkshire Railway because Manchester was one side of the Pennines and all the steel works were on the other. So Crewe had lots of railways joining and they decided not to build a station each; instead they built an island platform, which various companies' trains used in turn at the appropriate hour, signals permitting. Now in those days if you started off on some railway company you couldn't expect a through train from somewhere to somewhere. When you reached the end of that company's line you had to change trains and get into the carriage of a company who did go where you were going.

Anyway, Isambard Kingdom – I don't know what his friends called him, Issy perhaps – reached Crewe one day and found he was on the island platform. At that date they had not built the enormous steel roofed station that is at Crewe today with its bridges to other platforms. There was just this island platform with a certain amount of shelter to keep the rain off and on it was a refreshment room, because you were trapped there until your train that took you wherever you wanted to go arrived and took you away and the refreshment room was *de rigeur* unless you brought a huge hamper yourself. At any rate Isambard Kingdom walked into the refreshment room, because there was nowhere else to go and he had quite a long wait. He saw on the counter a splendid model of a locomotive called Lion, which had a tall chimney with a serrated top. The thing was about four feet long had six wheels and in the fire box was a methylated spirit burner and fumes came out of the top of the funnel, which was all very sensible. The women advised that it produced tea or coffee and he said, "Well, I think I'll have a cup of coffee," and she said "That'll be a penny." Now that shocked him because in Victorian England the proper price of a cup of tea was a farthing, however he produced a penny and she pulled a lever behind this engine and out came a dribble of some brown stuff. He tasted it and put it down on the counter and said, "Now I think I will try some of your tea." She pulled a handle and out came some sort of browny fluid into a different cup; he had to pay in advance of course.

He tasted it and put it down and examined a large glass fronted display case in which were some sandwiches that were a bit curly at the edges with something in the middle that was faintly green round the edges; it could have been ham sandwiches I don't know. The finest things on sight were some buns, which were beautifully shiny and glossy on top and had obviously been varnished with egg white. Brunel said to this good lady, "How often do you varnish the buns?"

She replied, "Once a week sir."

The quality of food at the Crewe station inspired the following limerick.

A gentleman dining at Crewe
Found a very large mouse in his stew
Said the waiter, "Don't shout, sir,
Or wave it about, sir,
The others might all want one, too!"

The Labrador Dog

Labrador dogs were first imported into Scotland, and I suppose the rest of Britain, by my great great grandfather. He'd shot everything you could shoot in Scotland. He was not responsible for shooting the last wolf or the last bear; somebody else did, but he got bored with the sporting possibilities of Scotland. He either bought or hired a ship. This was some years ago and it was a sailing ship but it had a funnel that you could haul up with pulleys. The captain didn't like lighting the boiler because it made the sails so dirty and there was always the risk of fire. So he set out to Canada because he thought the sporting possibilities might be better there than they were in Scotland.

I suppose this was in the 1850s or 1860s and in order to carry out his sporting (of course guns were not breech loading, they were muzzle loading) he had plenty of sets of Mantons (which were the best guns available in those days, cap lock not flint lock so they always fired even in wet conditions). Instead of having a pair of guns and loader as you would nowadays if you were going to a smart shoot, you probably had eight guns and seven loaders, each with a ramrod, a powder flask and shot and wads and everything.

So on this ship there's a certain number of game keepers and loaders and so on, and of course he had about eight hunters, a dozen coach horses with a couple of coaches and probably a shooting brake as well and masses of powder and shot. Oh, and of course a few retriever dogs, spaniels, etc. Anyway, he set out for Canada and he was very keen to shoot, for instance, a Red Indian or perhaps an Eskimo. But when he got there the Canadians said, "No, no, you can't shoot either of those. They're all citizens and you can't shoot citizens."

So he said, "What about some bears? I gather they're an absolute pest and kill people."

"Well," they said, "we'll give you a license for one grizzly bear and one ordinary bear." So he was a bit disappointed but nevertheless he bought the requisite licenses.

Mantons, of course, made nearly all their guns a sixteen bore, which if you shot straight would go nearly as far as a twelve bore, but they also had some little tiny small bore guns, which were really meant for people who collected birds and wanted to stuff them, and you loaded them with dust shot.

As he was wading through the muskeg swamps of Canada in September, the clouds of midges obscured the sun so he frequently held up his hand for one of his loaders to give him a small bore gun. I can't remember quite what they were – about a 32 bore or something. It might have been equivalent to a four-ten, full of dust shot. He would fire this into the cloud of midges ahead so he could see where he was going, then pass the gun back to be reloaded. But basically he didn't find the shooting in Canada anything really special.

He shot an elk (or a moose or caribou, I can never remember which; they're all the same thing) no Red Indians, no Eskimo as they were all citizens and eventually the time came to set out for home and immediately entered a thick fog on the Grand Banks. Now, as you probably know, the Grand Banks are a wonderful place for catching codfish and so it was covered in Dories, which were rowing boats rowed by at least two pairs of oars and frequently another chap at the tiller. Every single one had a big, black dog curled up in the coil of the anchor rope in the bows. During this thick fog his ship came to a halt because it was too dangerous to proceed and it kept ringing its bell every whatever the authorised time was, two minutes or something, and the Dories round about heard this and thought, "Oh that's a real ship. Let's go and sell them some cod."

After they'd bought cod off about six Dories, they said, "Thank you, we've got enough." But the Dories didn't have bells. They blew conch shells, which produced an audible warning of approach for something that seldom exceeded three knots, whereas the ship he was on it was fast it could probably do twelve under steam. He did notice in one of the clearing patches of fog that every one of these boats had a big, black dog lying trying to keep warm in the coiled up anchor rope in the bows. These people didn't use iron anchors; they just used a piece of rock. So he enquired as to what the dogs were for.

These Dories were all seine netting for cod. A seine net is a net that's kept afloat just below the surface and can be very long (depends how big your Dory is) but most people put out two to three hundred yards with a float on each end. This was a glass ball in a net of rope that was connected by a net lead to the net itself. The water there was so cold that if anybody fell into the water, he'd be dead in probably 30 seconds, largely from the shock. Because they didn't want to get wet and cold from the spray, they were all dressed up in sea boots and oilskins and that sort of thing, which would have drowned them pretty quickly too. Due to the fact that even in thick fog the sea still made the boats pitch and roll a bit they used these dogs. They pointed out and said, "Overboard," and away the dogs would go and grab the net lead near the float. They were trained to swim up-wind with it, which they did valiantly until there was quite a bit of slack in the net lead. These dogs had a thick leather collar with about three prongs going through the buckle and when the dog had got enough slack in the net lead, one of the men in the Dory would lean over with a boat hook and pick up the dog and haul the dog and net lead on board. Then he'd take the boat hook out and put it down and immediately take a couple of turns of the net lead round a – I don't suppose you'd call it a bollard. It was really just a piece of the boat – one of the ribs sticking up near the bows – so that if the boat pitched, the strain was held by the boat and not by the man. Every time the boat rolled towards the net, you could pull in a few yards of rope until you got the end of the net on board. Then you'd pass that back to the people further down the Dory and they'd start taking the cod out of it.

Well, when my great great grandfather had learned all this from discussing with the fishermen who were trying to sell him cod, he said, "Well, that's obviously a damn good sort of dog. Where can I get one?"

"Oh," they said, "well, nobody would sell their dog. There might be the odd widow perhaps on shore whose husband got drowned out here fishing and they might have a dog for sale." He went back through the very, very thick fog and eventually they put back into St John's because it was hopeless trying to proceed in such fog. They crept back at about two knots under steam ringing their bell and shouting and listening and they got there eventually and searched the town for anybody who would sell a dog. Eventually he bought one dog and two bitches, as expected, from the widows of people who'd drowned at sea and took them back to Scotland. They're quite different to the modern Labrador. I remember my grandfather had the old sort of Labrador and you couldn't possibly keep them indoors because if they got damp they stank. They had a very tarry coat and under it was an undercoat of thick grey felt which was totally waterproof but when wet they stank and had to be kept in kennels. Also, they were about twice the size of modern Labradors. A decent sized dog that you'd be quite proud of would be something like 130 pounds. My grandfather had these sort of dogs because his grandfather (who had imported the first ones) bred them and kept them, largely for the family but occasionally he parted with them to other people. However, they were very expensive.

It was well known that Mr Turnbull would swing across the line pursuing ground game and fire quite irrespective of the fact that there were a lot of people in the way and he would frequently pepper people's dogs. So grandfather said to Mr Turnbull, "If you shoot my dog, I shoot you. Is that perfectly clear?"

To which Mr Turnbull could only reply, "Aye mi'lord." Sure enough during some drive a hare or something ran through the line and Mr Turnbull fired at it when it was about a yard behind my grandfather, which is where his dog was sitting.

The dog yelped a bit and jumped to its feet and my grandfather said, "Right, I'm going to shoot you Mr Turnbull. Aren't you going to turn your collar up and turn your back?" Mr Turnbull fortunately had a very thick canvas coat. My grandfather had two cartridges of dust shot in his breast pocket. He'd put them there purposefully because he realised he'd drawn next to Mr Turnbull. From a range of about 40 yards he fired both barrels at Mr Turnbull's back. Of course nowadays you'd be had up for attempted murder or something, but in those days a Duke's son was more or less untouchable and anyway in the custom of the day Mr Turnbull was grossly in the wrong and deserved to be shot, and not necessarily with dust shot either. The dust shot of course did Mr Turnbull no harm at all; it didn't penetrate him anywhere.

Well the Labrador is still a good dog, but they've been bred so small now you can get them into the back of a Mini.

Highland Dress

Years ago there was an extremely rich Scottish nobleman who owned so much of south Scotland that he felt able to do things for the community, which he could well afford. In the middle of Queen Victoria's reign, roughly, he built Leith harbour, which is the nearest harbour to Edinburgh. In those days the North Sea was full of herrings and the harbour enabled trawlers and so on to tie up at the quayside with the breakwater around them so they didn't get smashed against the beach when the waves came roaring in. This greatly improved their safety. Before that they had to land their herrings on an open beach and anchor the trawler out in the open, as there was no quayside to tie up to and unload herrings. As the custom was, this rich nobleman charged a penny a cran – a cran is a box holding a number of herrings – many fish are sold by the cran possibly to this day. There were so many herrings in those days that there was a roaring trade. I am personally very fond of a good herring that has been split open, soaked in oatmeal then fried. It is a delicious Scottish dish, and kippers are very good too.

The city council of Edinburgh had different names to those in other cities and the Lord Mayor of Edinburgh wasn't called the Lord Mayor at all; he was called the Lord Provost and I think the rest of the council are called the Baileys, which is ordinarily the Scottish name for a schoolmaster. They were rather jealous of the fact that this very rich nobleman was getting a penny a cran for I don't know how many thousands of crans daily. So they put it to him that perhaps, as he could well afford these things, he might like to give them this harbour at Leith. As it was really a trifling expense to him, a mere quarter of a million pounds (nothing really) he said, "Certainly, of course, but you know there is a problem. I had to get the Queen's permission to build it as it's partly below the high tide mark, as harbour foundations have to be. If I'm going to give it to you it has to be given to you in the presence of the Queen and it has to have her say so. She is going to hold court at Holyrood House soon." So they made an appointment with the Chamberlain.

As you know, Queen Victoria was mad about everything Scottish, and in Balmoral and Holyrood House everything was tartan. Literally everything: the sheets, the loo paper, the potty under the bed. There were only three tartans in Scotland before Queen Victoria, but she said that every single clan must have its own tartan. There is a little shop on Princes Street, which as I'm sure you know is a one sided street which goes down into some gardens then down to the railway line. Anyway, at the north end there is a little narrow shop with three steps called James Hunter. Mr James Hunter was told by the Queen to invent a tartan for every possible clan; Mr Hunter no doubt made a good deal of money out of this. Many clans had never had a tartan; they just wore a plain woollen cloth, most likely dark yellow or dark green from a heather dye or another natural dye. Mr Hunter invented these square patterned tartans with the colours running at right angles, some of which were very complicated, but he still used the traditional colours.

This nobleman having made a date with the Chamberlain went with the Lord Provost and Baileys, all dressed up in their fur hats and gold chains, even though it was probably rather a hot day. There they were all waiting about when this very rich nobleman turned up dressed very properly in court dress. Court dress was white silk stockings, black satin breeches, a cut away coat with a white shirt (starched of course), bow tie and a top hat (that you couldn't wear in the presence of the Queen, you could only hold it in your hand, but it was part of the kit). I think he probably had a pair of gloves and a walking stick as well, both of which you handed to the servant. Once they had all turned up the Chamberlain took one look at this nobleman and said, "You can't attend on the Queen dressed like that! You have to be in full highland dress with your proper tartan."

Well, the Lord Provost and Baileys looked very disappointed at that because this fellow lived a quite a few miles away; he had a house at a place called Dalkeith just outside of Edinburgh. This nobleman said, "There is a difficulty here, Chamberlain, because the only tartan I would be entitled to is the Royal Stuart and I can't wear that because the Queen would feel it would be *lese majeste*. She now reserves it for members of the Royal family only. I'm descended from the Duke of Monmouth, who was the illegitimate son of Charles the Second. It's the only tartan to which I would be entitled. So would you not like to explain the difficulties to her Majesty and perhaps she will receive me dressed as I am, which is after all proper court dress."

"Yes," the Chamberlain said, "I'll go and enquire." This thoroughly intrigued the Queen and she agreed.

To this day that particular nobleman, whose family were actually my mother's ancestors, is still allowed to appear at Holyrood House not wearing a kilt and a sporran with a dagger tucked into his socks and all the other things like a velvet waistcoat. He is allowed to turn up in ordinary court dress. This holds with the present generation. I don't know how often the queen visits Scotland and summons noblemen to her court, but there it is. It's an exception. The Dukes of Buccleuch are the only people who are allowed to turn up at Holyrood House on a state occasion in ordinary English court dress. Although I think that's been relaxed a bit now. Our present Queen is very democratic and tailors are beastly expensive. When I was a boy you could get a good suit made at a London tailor on Savile Row for £150. Nowadays it costs £3,000.

The True Causes of the Outbreak of the 1914-1918 War

Most people believe that the assassination of the Archduke Franz Ferdinand at Sarajevo by one of those beastly Serbs called Gavrilo Princip caused the Austrians to start to punish the Serbs, and the Germans encouraged the Austrians and before you knew what happened everybody was at war. Well that might be so, but the fact is things had been festering for far longer than that. Now as every schoolboy knows, Queen Victoria had been on the throne for fifty years in 1887 so she held a jubilee. She called all the monarchs of Europe, most of which were her descendants, to her jubilee, which she decided to hold at Balmoral because she was much enamoured of all things Scottish. Now it was most interesting because at Balmoral the wallpaper was tartan, the loo paper was tartan, the sheets were tartan, even the pots under the bed were tartan. The guests arrived to stay at Balmoral where there was going to be a great shoot on the German principle, which Victoria had learnt from Albert. It was very, very sporting. What you did was you drove all the deer into a pen, which had high sides so the deer couldn't get out, and the shooters stood on raised stands and shot down at them from a range of thirty yards and none could get away.

However, the Kaiser Wilhelm the Second who was descended from Victoria's daughter, Victoria who married Kaiser Wilhelm the First, was the principal guest. (I always think of him as 'Villy vith the vithered arm.') Of course he wore a Pickelhaube helmet, which in his particular case, because he was the emperor, had an eagle on top of it which, if his ADC stood behind him and wound up the clockwork, flapped its wings. I wasn't there so I can't actually vouch for the veracity of that.

However, when he went to Balmoral he arrived rather late one evening and was told to go and have dinner in his room, as the kitchen staff had all gone off. So the following morning he was ready to come down for breakfast and he was wearing all his proper stuff, britches and gaiters and spats and boots, whereupon the Chamberlain arrived and said that Her Majesty would only receive him if he was in Highland dress. So he put a kilt over his breeches. He did look a little ridiculous, but then after all he was only German. He had to wear a tartan plaid wrapped around his neck and he refused to take off his Pickelhaube, but rumours say that he took off his sword when he was indoors (but that's only a rumour). Eventually when he was dressed to the Chamberlain's satisfaction, which was not quite as Scottish as some, he was shown the way to the dining room. Now on the sideboard in the dining room was a proper Victorian breakfast, which started off with devilled plovers, kippers, some kidneys, a bit of kedgeree and this and that and of course a great tureen of porridge. Whereupon Victoria, whose accent was still a bit suspect, said, "Ach, mein leiber Villy, you will some porridge gehafen?" to which he made a most unfortunate reply. "No," he said, "alvays I think as though a dog or a someone."

"Villy," said the queen, "you will go to your bedroom and you will not go to the Grand Batue." Now I for one am not at all surprised that twenty-seven years later out broke the First World War.

First Ploughing

Many years ago my grandfather was pioneering in Africa, which is the fastest way to lose the family fortune, which he did. He decided at one moment to grow wheat because it was all imported in barrels from Britain. To grow wheat he needed to plough up some land. So he got hold of an experienced Luhya ox-driver and about 16 oxen and a steel plough - very modern for Africa. He said, "Now look, I want you to go straight down there for three or four miles. There is a brown rock in the distance. I want you to head straight for that. You'll know you're going straight by keeping it in line with a particular part on the mountain in the background. Do you understand? You have to keep that brown rock in line with the mountain."

"Right," said the ox-driver. "I understand you."

"Right, off you go," said my grandfather. So the man set off, my grandfather jumped on his horse to see about something else because he had a lot of things going on at the same time. When he came back some hours later, he found that the plough had looped and zigzagged and come back over itself in curlicues and twisted and things all the way down to, well he couldn't see the brown rock because he hadn't very good eye sight, but as far as he could see. On the way back from the brown rock towards the mud hut he was living in the line was absolutely straight.

He said to the ox-driver, "What on Earth were you doing?"

The man replied, "I followed your instructions exactly sir. I kept that kongoni (which is a hartebeest) in line with the rocks on the top of the hill all the way, until I got a bit close and it ran away completely. After which I came back straight to your house here!"

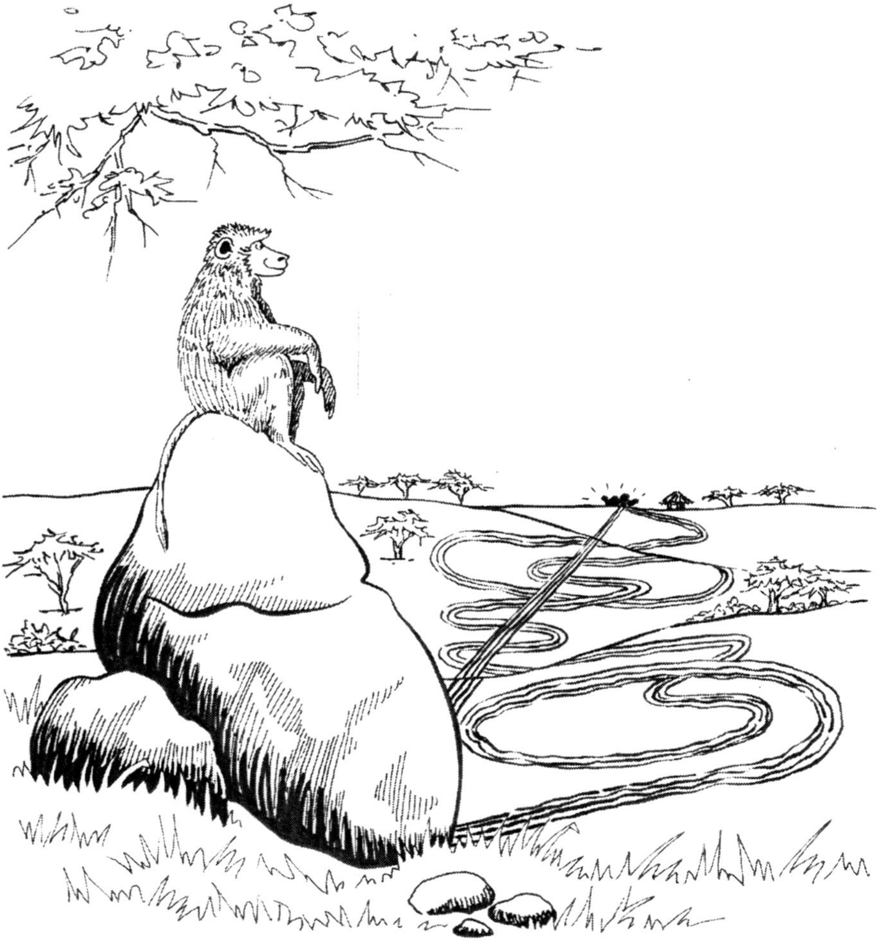

Colonial Railways

My grandfather lived in Kenya, as do I to this day. There were no roads in his day and everything travelled by train. Luckily he bought a farm near the railway. He had one or two problems with the railway. He used to go down to the railway every day to get his post, which of course came by train. One day he saw, in a sort of raised concrete platform with steel railings round it, three horses but they had no water and no shade. Thinking nothing of it he went and collected his post from the stationmaster, who was an Indian of the type I would describe as a babu.

There was one train every day and on the second day he again drove down to the railway and collected his post, if there was any, and he noticed the horses still had no water and no shade and one was lying down and the other two were standing with their heads down. On the third day he went down to the station again and he said to the stationmaster, "Look, if you don't water those horses and do something about them, they'll soon be dead."

"Ah," said the stationmaster, "it is not my fault. They're your horses now and you owe me three days demurrage." Now as my grandfather had seen him on all three days running he was a bit furious that he had not been given the consignment note and he suddenly remembered that he had bought some horses, four months earlier in England, and those were they.

Now there was no train coming, at least for the next eighteen hours, and he kicked the stationmaster off of the platform onto the rails. The stationmaster sent a telegram (the only sort of telegraph service that worked in the country was the railway telegraph service) to the General Manager of the railways, which in Kenya was a far more important post than a mere governor because the country existed on the railway. The telegram he sent was: "The Lord has kicked me, what shall do?" to which he received the reply within minutes from the General Manager of the railway, "Attend more closely to your duties."

The stationmaster eventually got his own back. My grandfather had imported a boxer bitch in pup. When she whelped he stopped the train just before the station by driving his buckboard onto the track because he wanted to avoid the stationmaster. But the stationmaster had a pair of binoculars and send off the following telegram to Nairobi where grandfather hoped to sell the puppies: "The Lord, one bitch, seven sons of bitch on train. No tickets. Please collect."

Rifle Barrels

Many years ago there was a plan to settle the Jews on a part of Kenya called the Uasin Gishu. It eventually was settled by Boers. My grandfather had recently settled in Kenya at the time and was very much against this particular plan and went and spoke against it in the House of Lords. What's more, the Jews came out and they looked at the land and when they found quite a lot of natives there with sharp spears and the odd lion roaring at night they said in fact they didn't think they wanted to settle there.

Nevertheless public memory was that my grandfather was very much opposed to this particular idea. He was busy trying to develop a farm in Africa and it included building water tanks, pipelines and water troughs and things like that, but he was always broke because he was very good at blowing the family fortune. He was looking round one day, I think he was reading the South African Farmers Weekly, when it said: "For Sale, Old Scrap Steel (Mauser Rifles)." Now after the South Africa war which ended in 1901 there was a peace treaty signed at a place called Vereeniging or something like that and all the Boers 8mm Mauser rifles, which were very, very long distance accurate rifles, were confiscated and handed in and put into a damp bunker at Pretoria where they rusted solid.

Eventually the wood started to rot and the government of South Africa, which at the time was British, had decided to clear this out, as there's no point in keeping old rusty rifles. My grandfather was looking around for some cheap steel, very cheap steel because he couldn't afford the price of reinforcing steel and he wanted to reinforce the walls of some concrete water tanks. So he saw this advertisement and sent a telegram, everything was done by telegram in those days in South Africa, saying: "I will buy a thousand of your Mauser rifles, but make sure they're marked as scrap steel because I can't afford to pay the duty on rifles." So the customs people in South Africa sent them as 'scrap steel (Mauser rifles).' They reached the port of Mombasa in due course, marked 'scrap steel (Mauser rifles),' and the duty was shillings per ton instead of pounds per rifle, which suited my grandfather.

The rifles arrived on the farm and were bricked into a water tank, which is still there, but rifle barrels don't go round corners so the sides of the water tank (which was square) were nicely reinforced but the corners unfortunately weren't. My grandfather knew nothing about building but he did enjoy dissipating a very large fortune. Quite recently one side of the tank fell down as it had come away from the other three sides so we put a big plastic tank in the middle of it. But this is digressing. I'm spoiling the story.

It happened that about a year after he'd imported the rifle barrels, there was a collier at Aden, which drifted in a gale and dragged its anchor and it broke the cable, which led down to Zanzibar in East Africa. Now the last three words that had been sent in a cable, actually from Kenya, read: "Help urgently required."

Now the foreign office aren't stupid nor are the colonial office and they quickly realised that my grandfather was about to do something nasty. So they sent for the customs department and they said, "Tell me, anything on Delamere?"

"Well," they said, "you know he did import a thousand Mauser rifles last year."

"Oh God," they said. So immediately a battalion was embarked from India on a boat. Of course you do lose caste if you cross the ocean, but nevertheless, bravely these sepoys got on the boat with their ammunition, rations, rifles and everything. Some of them were vegetarian and some of them weren't. Nevertheless they got on the boat, complaining a bit, and set off towards presumably Mombasa. When they got about halfway there the ship was equipped luckily with the latest Marconi device and what it said was: "Problem over, return to base." So this battalion in the middle of the Indian Ocean turned around and went back to wherever they started from.

What had actually happened was the cable had been repaired because the collier, having dragged its anchor, fished up the broken ends and spliced them together, covered them with gutta percha (ancient electric wire insulation prior to plastic), which was very fashionable in those days, and laid it down again. The telegram continued, having started, "Help urgently required," which caused a lot of trouble, it went on, "for famine in Turkana. People dying. Send grain." So they sent the battalion back to India but the rifle barrels are still embedded in this concrete tank, but they're not resuscitable into firearms.

Settlers Versus Officials

In the colony of Kenya, many years ago, the government was run from London and the settlers on the ground felt that they could run it a good deal better and often the two did not see eye to eye. In the middle of Kenya lies a great gash in the Earth's crust called the Great Rift Valley and about half way along it, not far from a spectacular extinct volcano, lived a settler called Gilbert de Preville-Colville. He had just paid to have a telephone line installed. This was a very modern idea. The line started at Naivasha, went halfway round Lake Naivasha onto his farm and up to the far end of his farm so he could contact his manager without using petrol (which was getting very expensive, it had risen to over two shillings a gallon).

Unfortunately the giraffe were taller than the telephone wires and they used to wander across and occasionally snap the telephone wire. So nothing happened for a long time and he'd paid for this service and was generally irritated. In those days the agricultural act provided that you could defend your property and your livestock against wild animals. These particular giraffe were Maasai giraffe. They're not rare or endangered or anything and in any case this was many, many years ago and there were thousands of them. So we shot them.

Whereupon one of the local officials from the games department got to hear of this and wrote him a letter:

Dear Mr Colville,

It has come to our notice that you are shooting giraffe. In future if you shoot any giraffe kindly send the entire animal in a railway truck addressed to the Chief Game Warden, Nairobi.

Yours faithfully,
Whatever the chap's name was.

Now this didn't go down frightfully well with Gilbert Colville so he decided to do something useful to make a bit of progress and all that, the sort of thing that the officials are very good at stopping. So he didn't shoot any giraffe for a while and Easter was coming up. In those days you could order a railway truck and it would arrive the next day. So he ordered a railway truck on the Wednesday before Easter. It arrived at Naivasha on Easter Thursday and he loaded it that night with six dead giraffes. He consigned it to the Chief Game Warden, Nairobi. The thing was hauled away on Friday morning because the railways work seven days a week, public holidays included.

Nowadays there isn't a railway which really works, not technically speaking. However, what happened was the truck arrived at the correct time, ready to be unloaded in Nairobi Railway Station, which had huge goods yards. Sunday nothing much happened but by Monday there was a horde of stray dogs baying under this wagon because the maggots were beginning to drip out of it and there was this lovely smell of rotting giraffe inside.

So nothing much happened until Easter Tuesday whereupon the Public Officer of Health had been summoned by the Manager of the Railway. Now the railway was a great entity in Kenya; it depended on the railway, and the railway was an important thing and people listened to what the General Manager of the Railway said. The Public Officer of Health for Nairobi was invited to send a letter to the Game Warden, which he did. Roughly, I can only paraphrase it because I never saw it:

> Dear Sir,
> A wagon consigned to you is causing a public nuisance. The stench is impossible in Nairobi Goods Yard. Kindly remove it at once.

No doubt when the facts were known to the Chief Game Warden, he removed the wagon and the railways made him clean it out and scrub it, which is all quite difficult. The carcasses, which stank by then, were disposed of somehow. The reason they didn't want anybody shooting giraffe was the Boers had a habit of shooting a giraffe and skinning it from behind one ear to the opposite back leg in order to get the greatest possible length of very, very strong leather and giraffe skin is extremely strong. They made what they called a *trek reim* out of these, which was used for tying their ox cart to the oxen or something like that. It was a practice that was more or less frowned on. However Gilbert Colville didn't bother to skin the giraffe. He wasn't interested in such things as *trek reim*. He shot them because they were breaking his telephone line. A few days later he got another letter from the local game warden that said:

> Dear Mr Colville,
> I have received instructions from the Chief Game Warden that you are not to dispatch any further giraffe to him in Nairobi.
> Yours faithfully,
> Signed (I can't remember what name)

The Whole Bible

The last ship into Mombasa, must have been about 1940, carried about 20,000 tons of superphosphate and a young man who was employed, from England, to come out and work for the KFA (Kenya Farmer's Association) and also several thousand gallons of methylated spirits. When the ship docked the young man from the KFA, or who was going to work for the KFA, was sent a telegram: "Divide the methylated spirits, one third for Shell, one third for Caltex and one third for Esso." Well this was all very well; he hadn't known what to expect.

He did that, he informed the people unloading the ship. It amounted to about a tanker each for Shell, Caltex and Esso. Nobody had sent him any standing instructions so he didn't padlock the outlet valves. He was due to get on the up-country train, which he did, and at the back of it were attached these three tankers of methylated spirits. In the yard at Mombasa were left the 46 people who died of methylated spirits poisoning because they couldn't resist drinking it and the quantities in the tanks weren't quite up to scratch. Nevertheless, he eventually arrived in Nairobi and – everything was done by telegram in those days – he received a telegram at whichever cheap hotel he was staying in" "Proceed to Nakuru and report." (Nakuru was the headquarters of the KFA). When he got there they said, "Right, the next three of four trains are going to produce 20,000 tons of superphosphate and we are sending some thousands of tons of it up to Eldoret where you have got to sell it because the War Agricultural Board is requiring the Afrikaners around Eldoret to plough up more ground to grow lots of maize and wheat for the war effort."

"Right," he said, as he understood. Whereupon the KFA got a telegram from Mombasa: "46 men found dead around tanker wagon."

So they attacked this young man and said, "Didn't you padlock the outlet valves on this tanker wagon as per standing instructions?"

"Well," the young man said, "I wouldn't mind seeing a copy of your standing instructions."

"Oh," they said, "I suppose you've just come straight from England without any standing instructions."

"Yes," he said. So they couldn't do much about that except they got another telegram the next day saying: "36 people have died in the Nairobi goods yard because they still weren't padlocked."

The young man said, "Well, you didn't even send me any padlocks so I'm shrugging that one off." The KFA director – I don't know if you remember old Norman Hardy and all that lot, perhaps you don't. At any rate he posted the young man to Eldoret to make sure all the Boers bought a lot of superphosphate to improve the production for the war effort. He went up there and was told to report by telegram monthly the sales of superphosphate and to whom.

When he had been there a month he sent back: "Out of 8,000 tons. Have sold 8 bags to the Anglican pastor to put on his roses and the rains have now started."

There was no reply from KFA so a month later he said: "Sales still remain at 8 bags. The Boers have planted their crops."

He got an infuriated telegram from the KFA: "Find out why the Boers aren't using superphosphate."

He said, "I shall need some funds to do spying." His salary was £5 a month. He was obviously a clued up young man. I don't know who he was but he obviously went far; he probably became governor of Tanzania. Anyway, they sent him 30 shillings for spying on the Boers. Now there was a family in Eldoret who everybody would meet and remember their name. If it wasn't the Potgeiters it was someone similar and the father of the family wanted enough sons to make a rugby team, which is 15. He produced 15 sons, or rather his wife did, although he may have had two or three wives, but the youngest one was a bit doolally and didn't always know which way to run with the ball.

So dad had to play in the team and they left out this young son and this bright young man from the KFA got him into a pub in Eldoret called the Wagon Wheel. He noticed that on the shelf at the back were two bottle of Van Der Hum, which is as you know tangerine brandy but there wasn't going to be any more coming in because the war was on. So he got hold of this young man and poured 30 shillings worth, which was the whole bottle, of Van Der Hum into this young man, while pretending to drink little bit of it himself, but only sipping. Despite the fact that this man was quite doolally and could barely speak English he wasn't getting anything out of him. The bottle was empty and he'd spent the 30 shillings given to him by the KFA. So at great risk to his personal

prosperity he said to the barman "Let's have the other bottle." He paid for it out of his own pocket. Brave young man, destined to go far. I hope he did well. The barman produced the bottle and he kept pouring the Van Der Hum into this chap who had a head as hard as granite as far as you could see.

Towards the end of the second bottle he said, "Well, there are reasons the Boers around Eldoret won't use superphosphate."

"Come on," said this young KFA chap. "Tell us all."

"Well," he said, "our Predicant who can read real good has read through the whole Bible from Genesis to Exodus and superphosphate is not in it nowhere!"

How my Father Helped Win the 2nd World War

My Father was born in 1900 and having not very much to do in 1923, he joined the Grenadier Guards. As their Junior Subaltern, when the Welsh Guards were reformed he was immediately posted away to them. When he reached the Welsh Guards, he was of course a Junior Subaltern and the colonel was a gentleman by the name of Chico Leatham. One evening at Mess, on Mess night, Chico Leatham mentioned a particular horse as being by a certain stallion and out of some mare, and Father, who knew a great deal about horses and went on breeding them very successfully until he was 79, said, "Excuse me Sir, the mare was actually (which ever poor devil she was)," and Chico Leatham said, "Young man, if you don't agree with me, don't talk at all." Now people were like that in those days. However, after a little while he left the Army and married my mother and did various other things until the war started and then he decided to join the Welsh Guards again.

Well by then Father was 39 years old and nobody knew what to do with him, so they made him a Captain, but they still couldn't think what to do with him. There was a very very top secret fellow called General Colin Gubbins who managed to find employment for him. General Gubbins was using the Home Guard because all the troops were busy either being evacuated from France or digging in or training or somewhere. Gubbins told Father that the Germans were going to invade the East Coast, either Norfolk or Suffolk or even Essex, but probably not Lincolnshire, and that all the roads leading inwards ought to be mined.

Now Father knew the area pretty well. He had a lot of friends there and had been shooting a great deal especially in Suffolk and a certain amount in Essex and a good deal in Norfolk. He knew very well the shore was all mud flats and you couldn't possibly get a Tank Landing Craft. It would get stuck and if you ever got a tank off it, the tank would get stuck. He did mention this to General Gubbins who promptly said, "Look here, you're a soldier. Listen to me and do what I tell you."

So Father said, "Yes Sir."

They started digging holes in the hedgerows both sides of the roads leading inland and into these they put a forty gallon drum full of Ammonium Nitrate and topped it up with a bit of Dieseline and then put a 2-lb gun cotton charge in the 2-inch bung hole with an electric detonator in it, which was led to about a 100 yards of wire. The whole thing then was turned upside down and buried usually under a Hawthorn hedge. Father did this as well as he could, dozens of them, Home Guard digging like beavers and any road of any size at all was absolutely secured with these explosives.

Father knew very well that when laying mines you had to make a map and so he made actually two copies of a very precise map with Ordinance survey – you know, 6 inches to the mile, very very well done. When he finished, he said to General Gubbins, "Here you are Sir, here's a map," and Gubbins said, " Is there another copy?" and Father said, "Yes Sir, in my briefcase," and handed it to him. Gubbins then burned them while he was watching.

He said to Father, "This is far too secret for maps to be sculling around you know. They might be found." Father was a little put out. After the war, as it happens, Father used to go shooting there again. Bear in mind he had sworn to the Official Secrets Act and couldn't give away anything but he did advise some of the landowners to tell their tenants not to plough too near the hedge. Well, that's only sensible, but he didn't dare mention it to anybody until he was 77, when he said to me, "You know all these mines, big 400 and something pound mines laid along the roads leading in from these mud flats. I just hope they are not going to blow up." But he said, "When I was shooting there about 20 years ago," when he was a mere 59 or so he said, " I had noticed some of the drums had rusted through. I could tell at once because if it was on a clay soil the diesel didn't penetrate the clay and it rose and killed the roots and there would be a big dead patch in the hedge. If, on the other hand, it was on a sandy or chalk soil, the diesel sank into it and dissipated with the rain, the ammonium nitrate fertilised the hedge and the hedge at that point would be about twice as big as all the other bits." So although he hadn't got the map anymore, he could still identify where the drums had been buried.

But the other thing Father did for Gubbins was with the aid again of the Home Guard people. Every single dairy farmer who had a milking machine had to have a little engine to work the vacuum pump, which is necessary for milking machines, and of course the National Grid and the Rural electrification scheme hadn't happened then so they had all these little engines, Listers or Petters or whatever they were. Gubbins decided that the right thing to do was to mount them on a concrete plinth, put some concealed hinges underneath and the whole engine could be tilted and that opened up to show a descending concrete shaft with a ladder in it. A few feet further down it opened out into a very large room, which Gubbins stocked up with all the things the Army were longing for like brand new Bren guns and rifles, ammunition, mortars, some mortar bombs, smoke bombs, flares and gelignite. All sorts of things. He was so terribly top secret nobody could deny him anything. This was so top secret Father couldn't tell anybody and of course the farmers who saw it happening were all sworn to secrecy as well.

Some of them didn't mention anything until they were literally on their deathbeds and then they would send for their eldest son and say, "Son under the milking machine, this is a very top secret thing."

The son would say, "Yes, I know Dad. The hinges were going rusty and I oiled them the other day. I looked down there with a torch and I know that the gelignite had started weeping and I'm not going down there."

Father would say, "So you know about it; it is top secret and you must never tell anybody."

The purpose of these cellars, which also contained food and drink, was to conceal the "stay behind" parties until the Germans were further inland, when they were supposed to pop up and interrupt the lines of communications and supply, block the roads and blow up bridges, until, hopefully, the first line invaders would run out of ammunition and petrol. All the stay-behind parties were volunteers, a very mixed lot, from retired generals to farmers.

Now, Father had been to school (it was compulsory) and had learned that the Romans had invaded in Kent and Sussex, the Saxons mainly in Kent and the Normans also in Kent. These were the only successful invasions. Nobody was stupid enough to invade the muddy, low lying flats of Norfolk, Suffolk and Essex, where the Normans would have been unable to get their horses ashore.

A man Father never met in the war, but employed in the late 1960s, Bill Binnie, was a 2nd Lieutenant in the Royal Engineers. He had been told by Gubbins to blow up Lowestoft Pier, and was provided with a three-ton lorry full of gelignite. Bill didn't think he would need more than half-a-ton to demolish the pier. It was doubtful whether it was strong enough to support tanks. Gubbins got very angry, and told Bill, "I'm a more experienced soldier than you are. I provided three tons, so use it all." Binnie replied that he would do as ordered, but that the excess of explosives would blow a lot of debris into the town of Lowestoft, and roofs and windows would be damaged.

"Shut up and get on with it," said Gubbins.

It was difficult for Binnie to find where to place all the explosives. He had been taught how to cut a steel girder very economically. He carried out the demolition in stages, starting, of course, at the seaward end. The first blast caused very little damage in the town. Those following came closer and closer to the town, and the damage increased. Bill secretly let the local grapevine know that damage claim forms were available at the Town Hall. Gubbins had been watching the blasts and the claims amounted to over half a million pounds. They were all paid by the War Office within seven days.

Now during this activity Father was billeted in a large stately home. He was billeted in the west wing of a large Georgian house, which was a nice upright thing with Corinthian columns and all that, or were they Doric, I forget. It had two Victorian curved wings added on and the owner had been longing to have it pulled down. Father went out to dinner one night and his Sergeant, who had laid all the mines and was very good with detonators, actually kept a box of detonators under his bed right next to a box of gelignite. He was very fond of these things. So when Father came back from having dinner in his dinner jacket, not in uniform, he found the west wing had gone. It had been blown up completely with the Sergeant. His host, somewhat senior to himself, was delighted to see Father back and said, " I'm so glad you weren't blown up."

Father said, "I have some difficulty because all my uniforms have been blown up and I've got to go and meet General Gubbins tomorrow and I have to be in uniform."

"Oh," said the chap. "That's perfectly all right. Come and have a bed for the night in the main house. I was in the first war and I've got a uniform that will almost fit you." So Father turned up the next day for Gubbins in a uniform that didn't quite fit, with the wrong rank badges on and the wrong regimental buttons and cap badges and everything! Gubbins, as you know, got a bit fed up with Father really.

After that Father was staying in a pub and the Home Guard who had been digging were sitting on a bench outside the pub and Father was in bedroom upstairs, but he could hear what they were saying. The poacher of the village, who was reckoned to be the best shot, and the gamekeeper, who was either his brother or his cousin, were chatting away quite amicably. All the members of the Home Guard were there of all various ages and they said, "What are we going to do about this Heinkel then?"

Heinkel? Now Father thought, "This is a bit worrying. My troops aren't authorised to shoot at aircraft." They had been issued with a rifle and five rounds of ammunition only and were only allowed to fire a shot upon an officer's direct order. Certainly they were not allowed to shoot aircraft. There was a lot of discussion from this bunch and Father kept silent and listened and they kept trying to tell the poacher how to shoot down this Heinkel. He was armed with a .303, which was a bolt action short model Lee Enfield, a very good rifle actually. They said, "You know, if you fire a round and one of your rounds is missing...."

"Oh, no," said the poacher. "I was at Ypres and I came home with a couple of spare pockets full in 1916. Very good stuff it were too. Goes very straight."

He said, "I've heard your opinions, like one of you said that I should wait till you say go when the aircraft is dead over the church, to fire at the tree over Parsons Meadow, but I'm not going to do that, I'm going to shoot at it just like I would a pheasant. I shall give it a good lead. I shall draw through it and when I'm just ahead of it I shall pull the trigger."

Well, Father got a bit upset because he knew that he couldn't stop them and because the Heinkel appeared suddenly. There was a sort of "Pop" from the .303 and the Heinkel burst into flames, landed about three fields further on with a very angry pilot. They all bicycled after him and the pilot spoke perfect English and said, "What did you do that to me for? I've never bombed or machine-gunned you. I've only photographed you." There was a Court of Inquiry, of course, and it was decided that no-one authorised the use of the ammunition that had occurred and therefore the Heinkel must have been shot down by a fighter that no-one had seen. So the whole thing was covered up with the usual military whitewash and everything was fine. Father quite liked that bit.

    Eventually Gubbins got totally fed up with Father so he was Returned To Unit, RTU'd! Which is more or less a punishment really. Gubbins was so Top Secret he went on to do all sorts of terribly Top Secret things, which I have forgotten. Nevertheless, Father returned to the Welsh Guards. He was then aged 40 and had no military experience at all. So they made him Adjutant to the Training Battalion because they couldn't think what else to do with him. It was rather sad. He was training up the sons of all his friends to go off and be killed in the Guards Armoured Division in North Africa and things like that. They were, too.

    He was based – well the battalion was based – on Sandown Racecourse at Esher. One day there were two defaulters. The Welsh Guards I should explain were mostly Irishmen because the Welsh were already in things like the Royal Welsh Fusiliers and the Sappers. The Welsh were most brilliant miners and far too useful to be put in a Guards Regiment. So they were mostly Irishmen – Irishmen always wanted a job because they were pretty hungry in Ireland and being big strapping lads made good Guardsmen. So the Welsh Guards were mostly Irish except for Father who came from right next door to Wales where his family job for about 600 years had been keeping the Welsh out of England. However he didn't mention that to the other people. So they managed to find some sort of employment for him.

    He had two defaulters one day. They were stacking reserve ammunition because it was known the Germans were just about to invade. They had sheets of corrugated iron bent into a semi-circle and they parked these along the roads and they then covered them with a bit of sacking and any schoolboy could lift the sacking and see what was in there; stacks of shells and ammunition of all sorts ready to resist the undoubted German onslaught. Later on in the war the same system was used before the D-Day invasion. Thousands of tons of ammunition was just stacked about in the open. These two defaulters were told to take a 3-ton lorry load of anti-aircraft ammunition, which is perfectly safe until you fire it, when of course the shell rotates which unwinds a little screw in the thing and then the fuse becomes live. Well that was the theory, but what actually happened was that one chap was throwing ammunition out of the lorry. The other one was catching it and stacking it, until unfortunately he dropped one. There was a very loud bang and the only thing they could find was a little bit of the engine block of the lorry and half a 10-shilling note. There was nothing left to bury; all the leaves had been blown off the trees for about 200 yards, a lot of windows broken, a lot of rather startled inhabitants of Esher. It was difficult holding a funeral with just half a 10-shilling note, but there was one.

While he was in the Training Battalion they had various exercises. They went off to Aldershot or Salisbury Plain, where if it was a hot day they were made to march and double march until they were sweating, and if it was raining they were made to dig slit trenches, whereupon the umpire would come up and say, "They're facing the wrong way! Fill them in! Go and dig them over there." A lot of soldiers had still got their issue Gas Capes and taken them with them, which people wouldn't have done later in the war. A Gas Cap is waterproof and if you cut four twigs you can hold them up over a slit trench and so long as the thing's on a slope the water will drain away backwards. The umpires will come along and say, "Hey, that's visible from hundreds of yards away. Take it down please. Roll it up and put it back in your pack." So they had a very happy time.

Eventually they got back to Birdcage Walk where as you know there is always one Battalion of the Guards Brigade. They were beginning to get the mud off their boots and one thing and another and hoping to dry their uniforms, when word came around they were going to be inspected by a General, not General Gubbins, on Monday.

Father had the most brilliant Battalion Quartermaster Sergeant who was really an excellent fellow who knew everything and how to get around all the difficult bits. He said to Father, "That's all right Sir, I know exactly what this General looks for. He always likes to inspect the toolkits in the lorries."

Father said, "My God, on this exercise we've just done, when one lorry had a puncture we had to search five lorries to find one jack and the rest of them to find the handle."

"Quite so," said the Sergeant. "There's a cure for this sort of thing. As it happens I'm friendly with a young lady who works in Woolworths and although it's now 6 o'clock on a Saturday evening, I know she'd do me a favour. If you can find me a quid," (and Father could find a quid) "I'll get her to provide 40 padlocks with two keys each and we'll padlock every place that these lorries have any sort of container that could hold spare tools and we'll padlock the containers under the back seats. You know, where the troops sit, long things they are."

So they padlocked everything in sight and this admirable Sergeant said to Father, "Put the keys in the secret drawer behind the big drawer in the Battalion safe. Don't let on to anyone that they're in there and when the General says he'd like to unlock the things to see the toolkit, you say that you're terribly sorry that the man with the keys is on leave."

"Oh excellent," said Father. So they gave the General a very good lunch. In the meantime the Sergeant had told everybody to scrape all the khaki paint off the wheelnuts and polish them up with Brasso and some Zebra Grate polish was applied to the sides of the tyres so they were extremely black and shiny. And everything looked marvellous. I mean the tyres were a bit bald, not much tread to be had, but then the Japanese were about to invade Malaya and rubber was a bit scarce. Never mind, the General inspected everything and thought it was marvellous and how very sensible of Father that they had locked up all the toolkits in case something went missing.

Well, after a fortnight or so they knew they would have to hand over to another Battalion. They rotated but the lorries stayed there and you handed them on to the incoming Battalion and Father said, "You know, I think perhaps we ought to open up these padlocks and see just exactly what there is and where it is and with this very good Sergeant who knows how to fill in forms in quintuplicate we could probably replace the toolkits and get everything a bit more tickety boo."

So the Sergeant said, "That's an excellent idea, Sir." They were just about to do something about it when the armourer came up, another Sergeant, a sort of lesser Sergeant, and said, "I've got some very bad news my Lord." He was always very punctilious about calling Father by his whatever he's called. "We're missing one Bren gun. I know the serial number and I am quite sure the Quartermaster Sergeant will know how to indent for it bit by bit, because you can't just ask for a new Bren gun because it is lost, not in enemy action. So what I think happened is that it is buried in a foxhole on Salisbury Plain that day it rained so hard. Do you remember, we kept having to fill in the holes in a hurry?"

"Oh, yes," said Father. So the Quartermaster Sergeant, a hell of a chap, indented. The first piece he asked for was one Butt Stock, which was a thing about three-and-a-half feet long and has the butt on it and the trigger guard and the guide for the return spring and the bit that the fore-body clamps onto. It was quite a large and expensive chunk of steel. That sure enough arrived and of course was stamped with the correct serial number.

Father asked, "How on earth did you explain that it got lost?"

"Oh, that was easy," said the Quartermaster Sergeant. "It was backed over by a tank, wasn't it Milord?"

"Oh, yes," said Father. Well then they indented for the fore-body and the stainless steel breech block, which is quite a complicated piece of machinery, and two barrels because they had two barrels; when one gets red hot you change it. You sometimes burn your fingers, but they have a handle which is meant to stop you burning your fingers, and then you had a pair of bipod legs and four magazines. It was quite a lot to indent for and he found really ingenious reasons for why the things had gone missing. I mean to lose two barrels just like that? Well, they weren't lost. The fact is one of them they said they were out on this exercise, it was dark and a lorry backed over the whole thing and it drove the barrel so deeply into the mud they couldn't find it. The other one, well, they'd been firing a lot of ammunition through it and of course it was red hot and somebody went and touched it and dropped it in a hurry, but they were on a bridge by the river and the river was too deep and nobody could swim. There were very good excuses for everything and they got, in about a week, a complete new Bren gun. That was marvellous!

Hand-over day was getting closer and closer and Father said, "Look, I think we had better get the keys to those padlocks out and have a look and see just exactly what we've got." So they did that and between the 20 lorries they had there was one complete toolkit, except the screwdriver was rather bent. But in one of the long containers at the back where usually you have six soldiers sitting they found a rather rusty Bren gun with the same serial number as their brand new shiny one! Now it's just a Court Martial offence that you lose a Bren gun not by enemy action, but if you have two with the same serial number, I mean it's hanging, drawing and quartering. It's a really serious offence; it includes fraud and forgery and blasphemy and everything. So Father, being the Adjutant, agreed with the Quartermaster Sergeant that he would dispose of it. The distance from Westminster Bridge from Birdcage Walk isn't very far; it's I suppose, a mile-and-a-quarter and Father was saluted smartly by the sentry as he walked out, but the funny thing is he'd developed a slight limp because down his right trouser leg he had one complete Bren gun butt-stock, old and a bit rusty, probably not very good for his trousers. When he got to about the middle of Westminster Bridge he found a rather officious looking policeman who obviously thought Father was going to commit suicide because he kept looking down at the swirling muddy Thames as it came under the bridge. Father said, "I'm the military officer in charge of Birdcage Walk. I'm the Adjutant and I'm just checking up to see how secure things are around here. Any aircraft today?"

The policeman saluted and said, 'No, Sir. All quiet, Sir."

Father said, "Well done, thank you very much." They eventually got to know each other really quite well because on succeeding occasions Father disposed of two barrels (he had to walk with a very stiff leg) with those slightly rusty barrels, not very good for his trousers. Anyway, he managed to slip them into the river and the bipod legs and the whole of the Bren gun went into the river but at the end of it all the battalion weapons were absolutely up to strength and they had one very new shiny Bren gun and so Father contributed a great deal to winning the second world war!

Marmalade

Everybody knows about marmalade. It's made in Dundee by J Robertson and you can have Golden Shred or Silver Shred. In fact, there are some lesser makes to be had nowadays, but in Robertson's heyday you got a Golliwog on every jar. However, Golliwogs are no longer politically correct, but it's still a very good make of marmalade and it comes from Dundee.

I was at school with two chaps who came from Dundee by the name of Maconachie. Their grandfather had made a lot of money in the First World War when the British government was desperate for anything on which to feed the soldiers and they were very short of things like jam. This old granddaddy Maconachie had the contract for sweeping out the moving picture houses in Dundee. There were two moving picture houses in Dundee, which I wouldn't say was the centre of civilization, but there were quite a lot of people working there and these picture houses opened in about 1912. Silent movies of course and black and white but well patronised and everybody smoked. There were no ashtrays, so they just stamped them into the floor.

This chap Maconachie used to sweep up all the cigarette ends, pipe dottle and matchsticks and things, and clean up the place considerably. He'd put them in a bin, then on a wheelbarrow and take them away. He thought, "Now that's all right, I'm being paid for doing this, but surely there must be some other way to make a little more profit." So he took to soaking the cigarette ends in water and produced a very strong solution of nicotine, which is extremely poisonous, particularly to things like greenfly which ate the raspberries around Dundee. Dundee is very famous for its raspberry jam and in the war there was a shortage of raspberry jam. The cigarette ash he sieved out of this mess, he sold to the raspberry growers as fertiliser, but there wasn't a great deal of it.

So he was left with a huge pile of matchsticks and he thought, "What can I do with that?" He suddenly had a brilliant idea. He bought himself an old second hand mincing machine, which wasn't quite as sharp as it was when it was new, and put the matchsticks through it. Then he went out into the fields and bought some turnips and some cochineal. He also acquired some sugar beet from the fields. He boiled all of this with some sugar and put in little bits of the chipped matchsticks and made, what he called, raspberry jam. He got somebody to tin it as there were already other people tinning things in Dundee, like Mr Robertson and his excellent marmalade. He sold it to the British government who were very grateful to get an additional source of jam for the troops. It was pretty disgusting but they bought it and when the troops complained they told them that it was all they could get and not to argue, discipline and all that.

After that he thought, "Well what now?" So he went round to all the slaughterhouses asking if they had any really cheap meat they could cut into cubes so he could make it into stew. They had a few bits of things left over, so they chopped them all up and he made it into stew. He then had this tinned by somebody or other, possibly Robertson. There was a problem in the trenches; if you lit a fire the enemy could see you and shoot at you, as this was the 1914 war. So he invented the self-heating tin as he had a friend who was a chemist. They had a little glass capsule full of concentrated sulphuric acid in a compartment below the stew in the tin and the rest of the compartment was full of water. If you gave it a good whack and bent in the bottom of the tin it broke the capsule of sulphuric acid, which mixed with the water. I don't know if you've ever been in a chemistry laboratory, but when that happens it becomes extremely hot. This produced a self-heating tin of stew. I don't think it was very good stew but the government were terribly keen to get anything to feed their troops, which wasn't actually fresh. They were very keen on tinned material as it would keep and could be buried and dug up again and didn't need refrigerating. So Maconachie did very well out of all of that.

Now, to get to back to marmalade, which, after all, is the title of this chapter. Marmalade was invented because of the impatience of some Spaniards. Now, as I'm sure everybody knows and every schoolboy has been taught, trade in the Mediterranean was entirely monopolised by the people from Venice and Genoa and nobody else had a look in. If you wanted to buy mustard you bought it from the Venetians who sold it at a very high price saying that it was hot because it grew directly under the sun on the far side of Arabia, which wasn't strictly true. At the same time you could get a China orange. Now, the fact is oranges did indeed come from China, but they were actually grown in Egypt. The Chinese had learnt a long time ago how to graft all sorts of things together. They discovered that the sweet orange, which nowadays is commonly known as the Washington Navel or the Valencia, grows best grafted onto a bitter orange rootstock. Bitter orange is nowadays called the Seville orange and it's what you make marmalade out of.

Some Spaniards who couldn't speak Egyptian or Arabic happened to be on a Venetian trading vessel and they went a little way up the Nile at Alexandria and found this fruit tree nursery there. Using sign language they explained to the proprietor they wanted some orange trees. He eventually got the idea and produced some little things about a foot high with just a few leaves on and they said, "No, no, no we want them bigger than that." He tried to explain to them that what they were looking was some rootstock, which he was about clip back and graft a sweet orange onto. They weren't having it. They thought they were being swindled and they said, "No, we want those tall ones," and they got them. However, what they got was a Seville bitter orange.

They took these back in triumph to the King of Spain. They bought quite a lot of them, a thousand or more, and said, "Look what we've got. We are going to grow our own oranges; it's no longer necessary to buy them from the Venetians." The king was delighted. After four or five years these things fruited and the fruit was quite inedible. Have you ever tried to eat a Seville orange? It's quite impossible to eat. The king was a bit disappointed but something had to be done with all these trees; there was a huge orchard of them.

It so happened that sugarcane was also grown quite widely around the Mediterranean, although it probably originated from Indonesia. It was grown in Italy and southern Spain, as it takes quite a lot of water and warm climate. So sugar was readily available there; it was fairly luxurious stuff by the time it got to Britain. The Spaniards discovered if they chopped up Seville orange, with the seeds taken out as they were very bitter, and boiled it up with an equal weight of sugar it made a sort of smeary thing, which they ate as a pudding. They were given a bowl of it after they'd had supper and they called it marmalado, I'm not sure why, but they did.

They hadn't invented how to tin things but I suppose there must have been times, when they weren't busy capturing Englishmen to burn them for the Spanish Inquisition, when the odd traveller said, "There's this funny stuff they have that tastes rather good." Somebody got, I presume, a stone jar of it with the top covered in beeswax to keep it airtight and brought it back to England where the people said, "That's nice."

The traveller said, "Well, it's quite expensive. I've been carrying it on a donkey the whole way from Seville and it was quite pricey." So they spread it thinly on bits of bread and it was delicious. The British have this habit today; they usually spread it on toast at breakfast time. However, Robertson's make more marmalade than they do in Spain.

Advertising

Advertising has changed a great deal in the 20th century. I haven't noticed if it's changed again in the 21st, but at the beginning of the 20th century advertisements were full of fine print telling people what a marvellous product it is and how many vitamins are in it and goodness knows what. I can give you an example of this. My Father had no income to speak of when he had just married my mother and found that when he was in the Welsh Guards his income wouldn't support my mother, himself and some children on the way. He resigned from the Welsh Guards and opened an advertising agency with a very clever Welshman called Everett Jones and the agency was called Everett's. This Welshman was a very cunning sort of chap. The idea was that Father, being a toff, would know all the nobs and introduce himself and say, "I can do all your advertising for you," and Mr Jones would think up the bright ideas, which he did. He would also organise all the commercial side of things of which Father had absolutely no knowledge at all.

One of the first accounts they managed to get was that of Bovril, which is a beef extract and comes in dark jars, rather like Marmite. In those days, which was about 1924, the thing was to tell everybody how nutritious it was and how many calories it had, vitamins etc. So Father approached a Home Office pathologist, an extremely famous man called Sir Bernard Spilsbury, who in the early part of his life had been analysing Egyptian corpses for arsenic and then getting whoever was appropriate hung. The problem with that is the soils in Egypt are riddled with arsenic anyway, so any corpse you dig up is full of arsenic but the neighbours got their scores repaid by saying, "Oh, so-and-so killed his wife. Dig her up, you'll find she's full of arsenic." Indeed it was so and so-and-so got hung. Sir Bernard Spilsbury was an expert at analysing for arsenic so he made a very good living.

Eventually he came to England where he was appointed the Home Office pathologist. When Father got the Bovril account he thought the thing to advertise is how good it is for you. So he sent a jar of Bovril to Sir Bernard Spilsbury and said, "Could you please analyse this for us?"

Sir Bernard said, "Yes, but it is £100 cash in advance." Father was right at the beginning of his career and had no money but he managed to borrow a tenner here and a fiver there from his friends and sent Sir Bernard Spilsbury £100. After a couple of weeks nothing had come back so Father rang him up and Sir Bernard said, "Well, I've got rather a lot on. I'm afraid you're still about 20 cases down." Eventually, after about three weeks, he said, "I've finished the analysis; I'll send it to you. Remind me again, what's your address?"

Father told him and when the analysis came it said: "Water 80%, salt 10% and the rest charred organic matter. Signed B. Spilsbury."

Well, Father reckoned he'd wasted his £100 and so did everyone else. However, the Welshman said, "That's £100 gone down the drain but never mind, the Bovril account if we can get it going will be paying us thousands. So stop worrying about it." He was a very cheerful chap and very cunning. He produced a drawing – they had a resident artist – of a brick well (in colour) with a Hereford steer jumping down into it. Instead of the huge description saying how good it is for you, it just said: "A little Bovril goes down well."

This was a complete new departure in advertising and was put up all over London and other places. Huge posters, about 40 foot by 20, made of dozens of sheets of stuff and the edges had to line up exactly or the drawing would have been crooked (there were fellows who were experts at brushing wallpaper paste, or whatever it was, onto these things to put them up). This went down very well and Everett Jones, who was Welsh, said, "Let's try to get the Guinness account." So they went to see the Guinness people who had very tedious advertisements. A bottle of Guinness showing with lots of descriptions saying made from the finest Irish whatever Guinness is made of (I don't think it's potatoes, probably barley or something), it's very good for you and its alcohol content is something or other.

Everett Jones said, "Alcohol content is a legal matter so we'll just put it in the bottom left hand corner. We'll put a bottle of Guinness only about 2 or 3 feet high, remembering the poster is 20 feet high, and across the middle of the bottom in bigger letters we will write: "Guinness. It's amazing what two can do. In the middle of the poster we will have a branch of a tree with two toucans sitting on it." So that is what they produced. "Guinness. It's amazing what two can do."

Well, this was success and Bovril and Guinness were paying them quite well, although Bovril weren't quite as rich as Guinness. Nobody had ever seen advertisements like this before. They had all been covered in fine print telling you how good your boot polish was, how it waterproofed your boots and you should brush it on twice a day; very complicated stuff, all the fine print that I never bother to read. If you're rocketing through a train station and you suddenly see, "A little Bovril goes down well," you'll probably remember it and think, "Bovril? I might try some of that." Actually, I personally greatly prefer Marmite.

Then they tried for the Nestlé account, which was a well-known make of chocolate. It belongs to the Swiss, but it's a very good make of chocolate. Everett Jones decided that they would have the silver paper of the outer wrapping drawn back a little bit at one corner and a picture of a glass and a half of milk pouring into this. Nestlé had been advertising that every one-pound bar of their milk chocolate contained a glass and a half of milk. So they did that, produced the drawing with very realistic glasses of milk pouring into where the silver paper had been opened. They hadn't completely stripped the bar; the packaging was mostly there saying Nestlé Milk Chocolate.

Then it came to the time to have it printed. Unfortunately, their artist was slightly colour blind; he couldn't tell green from purple. Now Nestlé had its own colour, I forget whether it was pale blue or royal blue or purple, but it was not bright green. While Father was out, the man had approved it. Everett Jones was away drumming up support in Birmingham or somewhere. Before anybody could say stop something like 200 posters, 40 feet by 20, had been printed in full colour. The wrong colour. Green.

Father came back. He'd ordered one of his minions to send across a copy of the finished poster to Nestle to see if they approved, and there was a Nestle man in his office stomping up and down waiting for him. He said, "This won't do, we don't have green packets. Ours are blue!"

"Oh," said Father. They had to pulp the whole bloody lot; I forget how many tons of printing paper it was but a hell of a lot. It set them back. Luckily by then they had a good turnover and a good overdraft, but it still cost them a bloody fortune having all these posters pulped. There was no point in keeping the plain bits because the man putting them up would get in a muddle as they all had little serial numbers tiny on the margin. So they lost a great deal of money on that particular one. It all came back later but it just goes to prove that you should not have a colour-blind artist in your advertising agency.

The Konigsberg's Last Shell

The Konigsberg was a German cruiser which mounted, I think, eight 4.1" guns and caused absolute havoc at the end of 1914 and throughout 1915 up and down the East African coast. It sank a British warship, a small one called *Pegasus*, in Zanzibar harbour while she was having her engines mended and couldn't move. I thought that was a bit unsporting, but anyway warfare is warfare. After that the Konigsberg captured several other British ships and took the coal out of them to keep going. There came a time when British ships were warned to stay away from that area and some warships were sent out to hunt the Konigsberg. They failed to find her because once she'd got dangerously low on coal the Germans had sent another ship out which contained a great deal of coal, thousands of rifles and millions of rounds of ammunition, all intended for General von Lettow-Vorbeck. He was a very good general who ran the German campaign in Tanganyika. Although he was outnumbered 10 to 1 by General Smuts he managed to keep going until after the end of the war.

When the Konigsberg sank, the captain dismounted the guns and got them ashore.

The Konigsberg I should explain had been lying up in one of the branches of the Rufiji delta and it took the British a long time to find her. The guns were dismounted, the ammunition carried ashore, some wheels were found to put on the guns. It was tsetse fly country and all the draught animals died like flies, so the guns had to be pulled by sailors. But I should explain how they found the Konigsberg.

The British Navy scoured the seas without success until it was decided that a little bit of spying and perhaps a little bit of bribery and a few inducements were needed. They asked the natives had they seen the

Konigsberg or a big German ship – she wasn't very big only about 3100 tons. Eventually some African from Tanzania (as it is now, it was called, Tanganyika in those days) said he had seen the Konigsberg disappear up into the fan of streams that form the Rufiji delta. He wasn't quite sure which one and it had been two or three months since he saw it. He thought it was the ship they were describing. It was definitely a steamship and it had guns and that was the best he could do.

Well, that left the British still wondering how to find the Konigsberg. So they sent out from England two 12-inch monitors. A monitor is a special shallow draught ship self-propelled by steam with one very big gun (or occasionally two) – 12-inch guns. These things could shoot a long way with a big heavy shell. I remember one of the monitors was called the *Mersey* but I can't remember the other one's name. They also sent out a seaplane tender with two aircraft. Mind you in 1916 the aircraft weren't very developed and were mostly made of cardboard, paper and string; when they crashed you just glued them back together again and they were perfectly all right. They moved so slowly you hardly hurt yourself. When they did crash you could pretty well jump off them when they hit the ground and you'd be quite all right. The parachute wasn't thought much of in the British Air Force at the time, although it was of course in the Royal Naval Air Service.

They had two Curtis float planes flown by extremely brave men. They flew all over the Rufiji delta until one of them saw the Konigsberg. Unfortunately, they were by then within rifle shot and the crew lined up on the deck and peppered away at these aircraft, which could fly up to 40 miles an hour (pretty fast really). Occasionally they just made holes in the wings, occasionally they hit something that mattered like the engine and occasionally they made a hole in the petrol tank, which was all very frightening. I believe one of the pilots was actually killed, but whether it was by bullet or by crashing I cannot recall. You could look it all up on Google or in history books or something.

The monitor's fire was then observed and directed by one of the planes. They kept gluing them back together and tying them up with string to keep them flying. They couldn't send a message by wireless and telegraphy as wireless sets were too heavy to go in aeroplanes in those days so they had an Aldis lamp, which was fine until the batteries went flat. They probably had to fly halfway back from the Konigsberg to where their seaplane tender or the monitors were to send the message. Nevertheless, in time several of the 12-inch shells hit the Konigsberg and she sank, but not very far because the water was extremely shallow and she was tied up right against the bank. She had been covered in branches of mangrove and stuff like that to camouflage her a bit, but it was quite obvious from an aeroplane that there was a ship. When she sank, her captain had the guns dismounted, taken ashore, wheels put on and dragged them off to join von Lettow-Vorbeck. They also took a great deal of ammunition, whatever was left in the magazines.

Von Lettow-Vorbeck was chased by General Smuts all over Tanganyika right down to the far end of Portuguese East Africa. It took a fortnight after the war ended to get a message to him that the fighting had stopped; it was over.

"All right," he said, "I haven't surrendered but the war is over. So I'm going to stop shooting you and go home." He told all his askaris, who were mostly Africans, to put down their guns and go home. He had no money to pay them with which was a pity but there you are. There had been a number of white German settlers, who were still part of his shutztruppe. Those who'd survived the malaria and all the other nasty diseases put down their guns and tried to go back to their farms in Tanganyika, but they had been sequestered by the British. Although after a few years they were given back their farms and they carried on farming.

In the meantime the surviving guns after this campaign – there were at least two still surviving on wheels – were dragged back from the end of Portuguese East Africa. Right back through British East Africa, which is now called Kenya, until they ended up at the ammunition depot at Gilgil, which is only a few miles from the farm upon which I live. Nothing very much happened there until 1954. The guns had been well greased so they still went bang if need be. Somebody thought it'd be fun to clean them out and to fire a few shells to see how well they went and if they were any good. They fired them into the lava flow, an absolutely impenetrable and uninhabitable lava flow, right on the edge of my farm. They fired about 10 shells or so but one of them missed the lava flow by only a matter of yards. It happened to be in wet weather and the soil was very muddy and soft. This shell landed and did not explode.

A herder who was wandering around there (outside the lava flow there is perfectly good grazing) found a little hole in the ground and he thought, "Well, that's odd. There must be something down there." So he poked a stick down it and felt something so he dug it up and carried it back to my house. It was a 4.1" shell that had not gone off. The nose of it had a funny little brass projection, quite small that looked rather like a stirrup. I've always imagined it was to make a delayed action fuse effect as it would crumple first to allow the shell to get through the outer ship's plating and explode on the inside of the plating, which seemed quite a sensible idea as the fuse that could be delayed set in milliseconds had not yet been invented.

At any rate, this sat on my veranda until the 3rd August 2014, which was one day short of 100 years from the declaration of the 1914-1918 war. The police came and took it away as they said it was live, dangerous and they must blow it up. So they took it down below the house and dug a pit in the ground. They put a little bit of gelignite onto it, an electric detonator and a long wire. Then they detonated this shell down in its pit to stop the shrapnel going anywhere. It made a good loud bang which I heard. It was amazing how well the Germans made those shells in 1914. They lasted until 2014 and still went bang.

Chinese Inventions

The Chinese have been civilised for a very long time. As you know, civilised people eat with chopsticks and not with their fingers. The Chinese had been cooking food nicely and eating properly with chopsticks for at least 3,000 years. They would boast to foreigners that their ancestors, while dressed in silk, were eating off porcelain plates a variety of dishes with chopsticks while the foreigner's ancestors were living in caves wearing un-tanned animal skins and eating lumps of roast meat that were burnt at the edges, if they were lucky enough to have caught any. The Chinese were definitely very civilised because they have developed such exquisitely painful tortures during which people would stay alive almost indefinitely in the most terrible agony. Hitler was quite uncivilised; he tortured people so badly they'd be dead in a week.

The Chinese did have one or two useful inventions and I love their stories of how they invented them. The Chinese invented tea, which is much drunk in Britain today (and in other places) and is grown in enormous quantities in Kenya. It used to be, and still is, grown in India and Sri Lanka. They drink so much tea in India that they hardly export any whereas Kenya has a massive surplus so exports tea very well. The Chinese story about how tea was invented has a certain amount of charm. There was a chap who wanted to be emperor, but he'd just lost the battle and his troops had gone away. I think the other side had bigger banners; you know the size of the banner is terribly important in Chinese warfare.

There he was, up a hill somewhere, hiding from his enemies. He was actually hiding in a cave as it had started to rain and to his surprise he found the cave was occupied by two quite harmless peasants. He said, "I'm the chap who would be emperor."

They said, "Oh well your Imperial Majesty, we are very pleased to see you, but I'm afraid there's really nothing we can do for you here. We haven't got any food because all these daft soldiers have stolen it. Nevertheless you can sleep on this sack which is stuffed with leaves here, if you like, and wait until it stops raining." So he slept on the sack stuffed full of rather pleasantly scented leaves. It had stopped raining by the morning when he got up and they said to him, "We're terribly sorry all we can offer you is a little hot water. There is nothing else."

"Well," he said, "that would be very kind. I would accept that with gratitude." He'd noticed that these rather fragrant leaves he'd been sleeping on had a very pleasant scent and he said, "I'll tell you what I'll do. I'll put a couple of these leaves into the hot water to make it taste of something other than hot water." Then he tasted it and it was delicious and that's how the Chinese invented tea. You can believe it if you like.

There was another fine Chinese invention, which I think is less plausible but still a good story. Roast pork. Now the theory of this is that some emperor, a different chap I think, was riding by when a pigsty, which was thatched, caught fire. The pigs unfortunately were burnt to death, but the most fragrant smell of roasting pork wafted across this chap's nostrils and he said, "That is absolutely tremendous. Now stop, stop."

So they stopped and he inquired what it was that smelt so. They said it was pigs kept in a pigsty with a thatched roof which had caught fire, and the pigs were roasted. Luckily they had some sharp knives about them so they cut him a slice or two and it was really excellent. "We had better call it something," he said. So they called it roast pork.

What I'd like to know, which rather denies the truth of the stories, why did they keep pigs in a sty with a thatched roof if they weren't going to eat them? Surely they didn't milk them.

The Modern Motorcar

When my Father was quite young, he was quite broke and having married my mother in about 1924 they set off to visit his favourite uncle who lived in Ireland. Now they had, of course, a second hand car because Father wasn't in the new car market. It was a Hispano-Suiza with a very long bonnet; they were wonderful cars extremely fast and powerful and if the length of the bonnet was anything to go by extremely fashionable. I mean they had a bonnet longer than a Rolls Royce, probably as long as a Napier-Railton all of which were very fashionable in those days. It had a rather peculiar body, which was perhaps why he was able to buy it rather cheaply second hand. The body was made of woven basketwork. It looked extremely fashionable and although it was second hand it was probably quite new.

Wonderful cars the Hispano- Suiza's; they had individual cylinders which you could take off one at a time, but I don't think you could drive them with one missing. It was so modern that it had independent rear suspension; that is to say a swing axle, which pivoted each side of the differential. Every time the car went over a bump, the axle would rub against the basketwork body and frequently set it on fire. My mother disliked that because in the back of the car was where she kept all her luggage and hat boxes and she kept complaining to Father every time the car caught fire that it was going to burn her hat boxes. But with great presence of mind he kept a Schweppes soda water siphon in the car and was able to extinguish the smouldering bodywork.

Father had developed a theory of how to cross crossroads. "The less time you spend on a crossroad," he said, "the less chance you have of being hit by something coming the other way. So the faster you go the safer you are." Logically that was entirely correct. Unfortunately, he drove my mother plumb into the side of a furniture van, that must have been when she was about 20, and bits of glass kept coming out of her scalp until the day she died.

However, the favourite uncle they were going to visit lived in Northern Ireland in the very far west in a place called Enniskillen. His uncle was in fact John Enniskillen (the Earl of Enniskillen). So the roads got rougher and rougher the further you went away from Belfast and narrower and narrower, really only suited for donkey carts. Just before they got to the house – it was a very elegant house that was frequently burnt down by the IRA and rebuilt by the National Trust. I think they enjoyed burning it down because there was nothing better to do in that part of Ireland in the far west. The house was called Florence Court; in fact my grandmother was called Florence, Florence Cole (the family name of the Enniskillens was Cole). Anyway, there was a little humpbacked bridge just before you got to the house. It was quite wide enough for a donkey cart, but Father drove up and the sump got stuck on the top of the hump, but also the bridge was slightly narrower than the car. The parapets closed in at the top in the centre and it jammed the running boards on both sides.

So Father said to my mother, "There's nothing for it. Climb out over the bonnet (because they were practically in sight of the house, it was only about another mile to go) and we'll find a local to bring the luggage up. I'm quite happy to leave it here, this is a dreadful road and the car (which cost something staggering like £12) has been such a nuisance we'll just leave it here."

They went on and eventually found a couple of friendly natives with a donkey and put the luggage on it, including the slightly charred hat boxes, and went on up to the house where they were greeted with rapture by the uncle.

He had rather strange habits, he would pare his sheep's feet with a penknife and then, without cleaning the knife, would pick an apple, cut it in half and give half to my mother (she wasn't quite sure about that). Anyway, they'd only been there two days when there was a creaking noise outside. There was in fact a gravel drive. Father looked out of his window and to his horror there were four donkeys pulling this Hispano-Suiza. "Sure your honour will be pleased that we've restored your motorcar. Tis a very fine motorcar, but the edges are slightly bent due to the bridge being too narrow." So Father was stuck with the damned thing.

Captain Sclater

Captain Sclater of the Royal Engineers was ordered to find a passable route to Uganda, in the early 1890s. Kenya was still called the British East Africa Protectorate. The Berlin Conference had divided up most of Africa into spheres of influence, later colonies, for the benefit of some European powers. Africans had not been consulted. Little of Africa had been mapped or surveyed.

Captain Sclater had been provided with a theodolite, a plane table (mahogany, brassbound corners, adjustable legs), plenty of paper in waterproof canisters, a tent, various other necessities, food and money. No caravan on foot could carry enough food to go to Uganda and back. No doubt the good captain had been provided with the British Army's latest weapon - the Lee-Enfield .303 rifle, issued in 1888. The short mode had not yet been issued, and the barrel of the Mark I projected beyond the woodwork. When a bayonet was fitted, the barrel could possibly be bent if the victim moved. Eventually, all the Mark Is were issued to the Royal Navy, who seldom used bayonets, which were, however, useful for opening tins, splitting firewood, poking fires, and various other purposes.

History has not recorded whether Captain Sclater wore scarlet or khaki. I expect it was khaki, but I'm sure he would have worn a pith helmet, or else a solar topee. No doubt he would have had a string of porters with a headman. Every item of his equipment would have been able to be broken down into 60 lb loads, the maximum a porter could be forced to carry. I should remind you that slavery had been abolished in Britain in 1807 and in the United States in 1867.

It is quite certain that Captain Sclater could not speak Swahili. He was about to pass through the lands of so many tribes that it would have been impossible to take enough translators for each one. Captain Sclater spoke English. But why was he ordered to find a good route to Uganda?

It was known from returning explorers that the Nile originated in Uganda. Britain had great interests in Egypt and the Anglo-Egyptian Sudan. Both these depended on the Nile. Uganda was known to produce cotton, of great interest to the wealthy mill owners of Manchester. It was also considered vital to prevent Germany seizing the source of the Nile. Perhaps they could have turned it off. If so, where could they have put it? British politicians may have supposed that the Germans could have dug a canal, and drained Lake Victoria southwards into Tanganyika. Due to lack of surveys, the relative heights were unknown. The Germans were, and still are great engineers. Consider the Kiel Canal, and the great dams in Northwest Germany.

Arab slave caravans had been visiting Uganda for centuries. Slaves were merely necessary to carry the ivory. The slave trade had been suppressed, but the tracks remained. Captain Sclater's expedition may well have been intended to be secret. I have not seen his orders. Was he told to find a route for a railway? Construction of the Uganda Railway commenced under Whitehouse very few years after Sclater's return. Parliament was divided over the railway, which was a very contentious issue. Disraeli was in favour of colonies, Gladstone thought them too expensive, and merely wanted exclusive trading

Rights.

After all, the British navy, the Royal Navy, was surely capable of preventing any German from trading with the B.E.A. Protectorate? But Kaiser Wilhelm II started building a navy to rival his grandmother's. That led to trouble that occurred after the period under consideration.

Captain Sclater set off from Mombasa, and immediately came to a ridge. "What is that called?" he asked. The reply was, "MIRIMA." It is on the map today. It means "hill."

As he trudged up the ridge, he felt it was time to insert another name. He pointed. "What is that place called?" The answer was "Mnazi Moja." It too is on the map. It means "one coconut tree!" Today the rest of the plantation has grown up. There are hundreds of coconut trees. As he progressed inland, he named hundreds of places, usually by whichever native name was easiest to pronounce. Frequently places had two or three names, if they were visited by two or three different tribes. He did not map the whole country, but merely the environs of his track, marking in such salient features as hills to make it easy to find his route. It was usually straight as long as the land was flat, or nearly so. In fact Kenya slopes upward from Mombasa to Nairobi at approximately 1 in 300. Nairobi is just over a mile above sea level, and slightly more than 300 miles from Mombasa. Beyond Nairobi there are all sorts of geographical complications: a range of Mountains called the Aberdares, and the Great Rift Valley, in turn full of volcanoes, nearly all extinct, but many still steaming.

One of them, at the highest point on the floor of the valley, is marked on the map as Longonot. From the edge of the valley one can look down into the steep sided crater, which is perfectly circular. The Maasai, in whose country it lies, call it "the black milking bowl," for which the Maa is "Lorok moti." Captain Sclater could not do foreign names, and Longonot was as close as he could get.

There are lakes in the Rift Valley, which he recorded as Naivasha, Elmenteita, and Nakuru. In Maa they are Nai'bosha, Mteita and Nai'ekuro. These are descriptive names, Nai'bosha means the place of dangerous waves. Mteita refers to the crust of salt and soda left on the shores as the lake evaporates Nai'ekuro means the place of swayback or spine disease, caused by a total deficiency of copper and cobalt. Interestingly enough, copper is required by all animals, and cobalt is required by the bacteria, which digest food in the rumen of cattle and other ruminants.

As he progressed towards Uganda, his way was blocked by a deep ravine. He pointed at it, and said, "What is that called?" The only objects in sight of any interest to an African was a mob of heifers, and the answer in Tugen was, "El dama," the heifers.

Blocked by the ravine, he headed back to the shallow end of the ravine, where he found another Tugen header standing in a characteristic pose. He was standing on one bare foot, the other foot pressed against the knee of the leg he was standing on. One hand held a spear which helped to keep him upright, the other a chewed twig, which served as a toothbrush. The ground was very hot in the absence of any breeze, and in bush country.

As our captain approached he removed his helmet, and wiped his sweaty brow with his scarlet bandana. Replacing his helmet, he said, "Tell me, my good man, what is the name of this place?" To which the Tugen replied, "Emening," having politely taken the toothbrush out of his mouth.

"Could you say that again?"

"Emening."

So on the map it is marked Emening. It is perfect grammatical Tugen, second person singular for, "I do not understand you." If a group had spoken the second person plural would have been, "Eminingiye."

On the map is Emening, correctly spelt, thanks to Captain Sclater, Royal Engineers.